Growing in the Spirit

James W. Tayburn, Author

Kent Banta, Photographer

Growing In The Spirit

Copyright © 2020 by James W. Tayburn

ISBN 978-1-7347100-2-1

Library of Congress Control Number: 2020909253

Printed In The United States Of America

First Edition

Publisher: Silver Millennium Publications, Inc.
            Gold Canyon, Arizona

"Not all that is seen is true nor all that is unseen untrue."

Jim Tayburn

Jesus told Thomas, "Because you have seen me, you have believed; blessed are those who have not seen and yet believed."

John 20:29

Acknowledgments

Poetry is something I enjoy writing and some would call it my passion. As a prolific writer over the last few years, my inspiration comes from three sources. First and foremost is the Holy Spirit. In my quiet moments, ideas often come flooding over me so strongly that I have to immediately go to the computer and begin writing it down. The second is the Bible. There are a number of poems in this book having to do with creation and I believe that is one of the main ways God shows himself to us. One of my favorite verses is Psalms 19:1 "The heavens declare the glory of God; the skies proclaim the work of His hands." The third is that my friends often send me ideas or suggest ideas they believe I could put into poetry form. It is not unusual in our discussions for one of them to suggest, "I'll bet there is a poem in there somewhere." I am so honored to have wonderful friends who value my work to such an extent. Friends are the stirring rod of all that life has to offer and I am so thankful for those who've been part of my life.

Many thanks go to Larry Newman, President of Silver Millennium Publications, Inc without whose help in handling the many tasks required for publishing, this book would not be in print.

A special note of gratitude goes out to Kent Banta, a great friend, a talented artist, and a wonderful photographer whose pictures are included in this book and on the front cover. Nothing delivers a message better than a picture, especially one that coordinates well with a poem. I'm so grateful to Kent for his invaluable help in putting this book together.

Lastly, heartfelt thanks goes out to my wife, Marie, who has worked side by side with me in all of the detail work involved in putting this book together. She has been the driving force in bringing this book to fruition.

Introduction

I've written poems for most of my life and I'd like to think they've gotten better over the years. You can be the judge of that. There are three criteria for my poems—that they rhyme, that they deliver a message for living, and that they honor God. My hope is that at least one poem in this collection will have meaning for you personally.

Never underestimate the value of family or great friends. Without their encouragement and support, this book would not have been possible. Each one of us has a gift and I would encourage you to find yours. Despite any reservations you might have, pursue it with passion. That's what God intends for you.

If you have been moved in any way by one of these poems, I would ask that you pass the book along to someone you know who may need a spiritual lift. Perhaps by this simple act, you can be a part of The Great Commission in bringing others to our only hope--- that is Christ.

Table of Contents

A Call to Action

Numbered are our days
Sands rush through the hourglass
Time is short to change our ways
Years ahead defer to years past

Without exception all men are lost
Only one way leads to eternal worth
The River Jordan we all must cross
And leave our material wealth here on earth

Time is wasting; listen, be still
His voice will whisper in your ear
Exhorting you to submit to His will
The days pass; His Spirit is near

Life doesn't have to end when we leave this earth
Jesus gave us a path to eternity with Him
Accept the Holy Spirit, an exciting new birth
And ask for forgiveness for all your sins

The call has gone out to change our behavior
The day of Judgment is around the bend
Take action today to make Him Lord and Savior
And begin your life anew with Him!

Author of Our Salvation

An ambiguous beginning—"It was the best of times and the worst of times"
There's great truth, even today, in Dickens' opening lines
While we work so hard to keep up with technology's frenetic pace
Ethically, morally, and spiritually we're falling from grace

We have every convenience to accomplish more each day
The answers to all of our questions just an I-phone away
That carry-around computer is like a helpful little elf
And we're not far from owning a car that drives itself

But we have lost our day of rest and Sunday gatherings at church
There's no downtime from our online social media search
Like the unhandyman, our socializing is awkward; we're all thumbs
How are we going to respond to each other when the crisis comes?

The online package will soon arrive by drone right to our door
Check-out counters are becoming a thing of the past at our grocery stores
But technological fraud lingers at every corner just waiting to pounce
Running up charges on our charge cards or draining our accounts

We can communicate with family instantly from anywhere on earth
And share in the excitement of a graduation, wedding or birth
But we've lost the connections and involvement we had before
Love your neighbor, but do we even know the person next door?

We were in awe when a team of doctors replaced the first human heart
But doctors today routinely replace knees, hips, and most other body parts
We're still the richest nation on earth, some with incredible wealth
But there are millions of poor who have no access to even basic health

The practice of law, at its best, provides for adjudication of grievances and correction
But today we are so sensitive and greedy that law has taken a different direction
Lawyers unapologetically advertise and follow the ambulance wake
Suing doctors who do ground-breaking surgery, for even the smallest mistake

Our system of government and way of life is the envy of the world
And yet there are those who refuse to stand when our flag is unfurled
Our free enterprise system has led to an unparalleled standard of living
Yet many game the system, happy to live off those doing the giving

We talk to our computers, they have names, and they talk back
But as far as conversing with each other, we may have lost the knack
The family unit, put together by Our Father, is fractured and dispersed
Humanistic answers and attitudes have replaced the God of the Universe

Countries compete at the Olympics as if we're all brothers and friends
But are likely at war psychologically or even militarily at games' end
Technology is supposed to free up our time, make us much less stressed
But we find new ways to burden our time and add to our distress

We're the land of liberty, pursuit of happiness, and free speech
But we shout each other down on our campuses and on our streets
Our schools are supposed to be safe zones for kids to associate and learn
But the disenfranchised bring guns to school when there's nowhere to turn

So where are we to turn to find the answer, reset our direction?
It's an answer most don't want to hear, this source of correction
Open the Bible, starting on page one read through to Revelation
God is our only hope, the truth, and the author of our salvation.

A Great Big Heart

'Twas the night before Christmas – midnight I think
When I slipped down the stairway to get a drink
Some clatter in the family room I suppose I heard
Instinctively, to the Christmas tree I was lured

When, what did my eyes in amazement behold
Not Santa and his goodies, as we've been told
But a slimy, green creature – a smelly stench
You know the one, the mean ol' Grinch

I watched in disbelief as he plucked from our socks
All the pontookas, bamboogles, and tocks
He lifted the gamboozos, the flitters and flings
The whirlybird zingers and all the other things

Everything was snatched off the tree in a flash
I held on to my wallet for fear of my cash
I did my best to hide my loathing and fear
Which he bolstered with his wicked little sneer

Then, as he turned from his dastardly deed
The last thing he stole was our Christmas tree
Up the chimney it went as he beat a hasty retreat
Hurrying to our neighbor's house just down the street

The Grinch took everything of material value that day
But our Christmas will still be wonderful, more than OK
For there is one thing I know he overlooked
It's there, deep in our heart, if we just take a look

The Grinch cannot make off with our Christmas joy
Because it's not found in any of the trappings or toys
It's a gift that cannot be stolen or taken away
It's the gift of our Lord Jesus, born on this day

It's the love of family and our closest friends
A love with a beginning, but never an end
No matter what life throws at us or how we react
These are the people who always have our back

So if there's a Grinch who's stealing your joy
Don't let him your Christmas spirit destroy
Stay close to those whose love you share
Maybe even offer the Grinch a word of prayer

We all know a Grinch, though he's probably not green
And I'd guess not nearly as vile nor half as mean
Though he may come with a large dose of "Bah, Humbug"
His heart can change with "Merry Christmas" and a simple hug

So don't give up on your Grinch, as you just might see
All those presents returning to your Christmas tree
Your kindness might just be the impetus, the jumpstart
The beginning of your Grinch growing a great big heart.

A Million Santas

So how does Santa do it—deliver millions of gifts all in one night
Seems impossible, even with a sled on a supersonic flight
We all know there must be some kind of magic involved
But I think I've figured out how this mystery is solved

First of all, I think we're absolutely right about the magic part
And we know from childhood that our Santa has a great big heart
But I don't think it's one Santa who's making the nightly rounds
But rather a million Santas showing their love in a million towns

Their itinerary does not involve reindeer, elves, or a million houses
But rather gifts of love to friends, children, and spouses
No rooftop landings, no red suit, and no chimney slide
But there may be a ho, ho, ho and joy they can't hide

Their gifts are not made at the North Pole by some elf
They're selected carefully online or from a store shelf
These Santas have commonality, though, at the Christmas rush
You can be sure they'll all greet you with "Merry Christmas"

You see these Santas are the ones who live every day with us
They're family or loved ones who we adore and trust
They embody what God taught us for those who believe
That it's far more joyous to give than it is to receive

There's a delight in giving that they bring every Christmas Eve
So please don't do away with the notion of Santa and disbelieve
The magic is that he's been there beside you all along
And believing in him at Christmas just cannot be wrong

So this Christmas, just enjoy the Santa who lives at home
He will never disappoint you and you'll never feel alone
The bag he carries on his shoulder is filled only with love
And it's more precious than any toy you can think of.

A Place on the Ark

Maybe they thought he was building a new living space
When he started cutting down cypress trees at a furious pace
Did they marvel at how logs were muscled to the top of the hill?
And why they did this hard labor with such passion and will?

Maybe they just thought he was a crazy old man
When they began to realize the size of his plan
I'd guess they ridiculed him and called him names
And yet he persisted with his work all the same

Maybe they laughed that his boat was not near any lake or ocean
And a ship with no rudder seemed like a ridiculous notion
And most probably didn't think the vessel would even float
After all, he was not any kind of shipbuilder of note

And yet he persisted with his work faithfully year after year
The scoffers must have had their doubts as the finish was near
I wonder how many were standing nearby when the rains came
And how many were clamoring at the door, calling on God's name

I'm sure Noah was praising the Lord as the water lifted the boat
And he realized for the first time the craft would actually float
The months that passed must have had its share of trauma
The needs of so many animals, the endless water, and family drama

The tossing and rolling of the ship up, down, and about
Must have created, even in this most ardent believer, some doubt
But the waters subsiding finally brought with it great relief
Especially when the dove returned with a beak full of leaf

God had saved the only true believers on earth
And had tested their faith for all it was worth
When exiting the ark and dropping to their knees, I'd guess
They undoubtedly thanked the Lord for how they'd been blessed

Noah and his family were the second coming of Adam and Eve
God had started over with the only ones on earth who believed
And isn't it happening all over again with the way we live today?
Are you one of those God will rescue on the final Judgment Day?

Or will you be part of the chaos of the masses as the door closes?
Begging to be saved, but not believing anything the Lord discloses
The time is now to acknowledge Him as king; come in from the dark
Because if you do, you'll be secure and have a place on the ark.

A Poet's Rendition of Ecclesiastes 3

There's a time under heaven for everything
And each season will a new life circumstance bring

A time to laugh and a time to cry
A time to be born and a time to die

A time for sitting out and a time to dance
A time for work and a time for romance

A time for holding back and a time to be bold
A time for youth and a time for old

A time to be strong and a time to be weak
A time to be silent and a time to speak

A time for business and a time to retire
A time to lay back and a time to inspire

A time for water and a time for wine
A time for the physical and a time for divine

A time to walk and a time to run
A time to be serious and a time for fun

A time for strangers and a time for friends
A time to save and a time to spend

A time for the rich and a time for the poor
A time for less and a time for more

A time to stand tall and a time to take a knee
A time for discipline and a time to be free

A time to stay and a time to roam
A time for gathering and a time to be alone

A time to receive and a time to give
A time to admonish and a time to forgive

There's a time under heaven for God's perfect plan
And the plan will be unique for every woman and man.

A Poet's Rendition of the 23rd Psalm

The Lord is my shepherd, my rock
I'm content to be one of His flock
He's always there to lead me; I know His voice
I'm compelled to follow, I have no choice

I shall never be in want nor want more
As long as Christ is there to go before
I trust the Good Shepherd in all His ways
He will provide for me, forgive me, and amaze

He makes me lie down in pastures green
He quiets my fears, seen and unseen
The presence of the Master fills my soul
I can release all my worries to His control

He leads me beside the waters still and deep
I'm at peace as one of His sheep
He guides me in the Way, the path of right
The lamp at my feet unmistakable and bright

Even in Death's shadow I have no fear
My Lord's comforting presence is always near
His authority is unquestioned; I have to obey
I'm under His protection tomorrow and today

He prepares a grand table just for me
Right there in front of my worst enemy
As His honored guest I am all aglow
The blessings are so numerous they overflow

Surely, my lot will be goodness and love
Directly from the Heavenly Father above
He will not leave my side, now or ever
And I shall dwell in His house forever.

A Walk in the Rain

What is it about running water that so enthralls?
Is it an adjunct of nature that seems to quietly call?
What is it that gives us a sense of calm and peace
Allowing us to just lay back and our worries release?

Why is it almost mystic to stroll along the ocean?
Or standing next to Niagara Falls, like a love potion?
Why does an all-day rain cleanse not only earth
But also refresh our longing soul, like a rebirth?

Given a choice between running water or water that's still
A dog will drink from the fountain until he gets his fill
There's just something tantalizing about water that moves
It's a great mystery as to why is so attracts, why it soothes

We have very little rain here in this desert clime
We're blessed with sunshine nearly all of the time
And when it rains, it's usually a torrential downpour
Accompanied by thunder and lightning—a lion's roar

But this week I was able to take a walk in a gentle rain
It reminded me of Fred Astaire's happy, sloshing refrain
Dancing and splashing about with umbrella in hand
Expressing a joy that only a child seems to understand

But as I walked with the rain softly floating down
It was if the running water had silenced all sound
Not only that, but all my cares vanished into thin air
And I could sense nature's revival everywhere

The smoky clouds made it seem like the mountain was on fire
One could not help but pause and for just a minute, admire
An amazing scene that only God could put together
Somehow, the rain just seemed to make everything better

This fast-paced world isn't one to provide solace
To realize the peace God so clearly promised
But when it rains again in a slow, drizzling way
I'll be in my raincoat and the walk will make my day

I'm sure many of you might think I am totally nuts
After all, isn't this weather why God made ducks?
But before you laugh and hold me in utter disdain
Put away your doubts and take a walk in the rain.

All the Love I Have to Give

I'm not strong, but I'm not weak
I can't talk, but I can speak
I show love in many ways
A love I'll show you all my days

I will always want to walk with you by my side
When I'm with you, there's a joy I cannot hide
Playing games or maybe just running free
The best times involve only you and me

There are times I know when you'll treat me bad
But you'll still be the best friend I've ever had
My dreams will be our activities in reminisce
And I'll wake you each day with a morning kiss

There will be times when I make you laugh
When my antics are just plain silly and daft
When I do my best to bring out your inner child
And even on a rough day, make you smile

I will show off my cuteness in ways you can't imagine
You'll feel obligated to take my picture again and again
When I'm asleep I'll be a poster child for peace
Helping you each day your worries to release

Who is this that is able to do all these wonderful things?
Whose presence can make a hurting heart sing
Who's more comforting than the warmth of a burning log
Magical powers these are, from your loving dog

My love for you has no limit, it's unconditional
So strong it is, it's almost inexplicable
But I'll be here with you as long as I live
Showering you with all the love I have to give.

Ambassadors for Christ

Because non-believers are lost,
We Christians have a job to do.

Because non-believers have a choice,
We must make Christ the only choice.

Because non-believers can be sensitive,
We must respect their feelings.

Because non-believers have questions,
We must have wisdom.

Because non-believers are unique,
We must be adaptable.

Because non-believers are searching for meaning,
We must be responsive.

Because non-believers have needs
We must be willing to serve

Because non-believers may be slow to trust
We must be a friend.

Because non-believers have influence,
We have the hope of others coming to Christ.

Because non-believers must understand His sacrifice
We have to be ambassadors for Christ.

America's Blessings

Lord, we look around the world and bear witness
The devil's work causing such distress
Starvation in Somalia; war in the Sudan
Turmoil in the Middle East and Afghanistan

People bathing in open sewers; sleeping on dirt
Nagging hunger; physical and emotional hurt
Families torn apart by war and strife
Struggling to have any semblance of life

Then there's us, Lord, in the USA
Sheltered in warmth; not hungry a day
Hot water and TV's considered a given
Autos and stereos – necessities to livin'

Freedoms of life and liberty a sacred trust
Though we did not earn them; considered a must
Democratic government; religious choice
The right to assemble and raise a voice

Lord, we don't know why you chose this land to bless
Giving us an abundance of all the best
But, on this Thanksgiving, we just want to say
Thank you for all the blessings sent our way

The material things – like houses and clothes
Produce galore – rows upon rows
The intangibles – like friends and health
And, comparatively speaking, our incredible wealth

But, most of all, Lord, it is on this day
That we'd like to thank you in a much different way
Not for material things – by themselves such a waste
But for the awesome power of your unending grace.

Are You Swimming Upstream?

Why does it seem we all like to swim upstream?
What's the allure; what's the goal, the dream?
There must be something more than a childish wish
To make us follow the example of a salmon fish

There's not only the power of the raging water to overcome
There are barriers to jump over and even death to some
What prevents us from giving in and just letting go?
Why can't we just lay back and go with the flow?

I think all this effort comes from a kind of macho role
Leave it all up to us; we need to be in control
I'll just keep on stroking, no matter the outcome
I'll only look for help when there's nowhere to run

But watch what happens if we admit it's not up to us
Life is so much easier if we just step off the struggle bus
God said know that I am God and be still
I'm God and you're not; stop fighting my will

I have plans for your life, plans that will prosper you
Haven't I already shown you how much I love you?
Release your grip and I'll take you through the wake
To where the water glasses out to a peaceful lake

When you finally admit that it's me in control
When you acknowledge that I touch your very soul
When you freely accept me and your burdens release
Then you will know what it feels like on that lake of peace

You were never meant to be a salmon, splashing about
Before you exhaust yourself and completely burn out
Reach out to me and we'll walk this walk together
And you'll know this life of yours can be so much better.

At the Doorstep

At the doorstep, agonizingly short on earthly years
Looking at a life woefully short of the mark
Hoping your promises will overcome my fears
That the ramp will be lowered to your spiritual ark

I know nothing of the crossing ahead of me
I pray the Evil One awaits not on the other side
All I have to offer is a life of sin and inconsistency
Your love traded for an inflated sense of pride

I'm completely at your mercy, a lost sheep
There's nothing at all I can do to secure my place
My sins are plentiful, embarrassing, and deep
I'm totally reliant on your forgiveness and grace

I envision myself coming weakly before your throne
Falling on my knees, too embarrassed to raise my head
I look for support, but this is a trip I must make alone
I deserve eternity in Hell, but I yearn for heaven instead

I know I should have focused less on the things of earth
And as you watched, I know you must have wept
I am naked, nothing do I bring forward of any worth
My days are numbered and I stand at the doorstep

The hours grow shorter with each passing day
Each day I approach closer to the Great Unknown
All that's left now is to accept your judgment and pray
That when that time comes, you'll welcome me home.

Attitude of Gratitude

Most Americans have material blessings beyond compare
When we look into our cupboards, they're never bare
When night falls, we never worry about where we'll sleep
Or the safety of our children in a world increasingly bleak

We have more than one car and a garage to park them in
And every couple of years, we buy a new one again
Our savings and checking accounts are never empty
Our closets have shoes, clothes, and jackets aplenty

Our houses are bigger and furnished with every amenity
We send our kids off to college to find their own identity
We can afford insurance for almost every eventuality
And we keep up with most forms of new technology

With all of this affluence, we're just one paycheck from disaster
As a result, we never find the peace and security we're after
We've forgotten that all of our earthly assets are not our own
And they won't matter at all the day the Lord calls us home

Instead of being grateful for the blessings we've been given
Or the fact that through Christ our sins have been forgiven
We go through life trying to keep it all under control
And in the process, lose all concern for the health of our soul

People with so much less seem thankful all the more
Wanting in material wealth, in spirit, they're never poor
They're just ever thankful that God sent His only Son
To provide a path to Him when life on earth is done

So, this Thanksgiving, what shall we do to effect a change?
Can we focus less on the material and our priorities rearrange?
Can we thank Him for our blessings; create a change in attitude?
Isn't it time we go to the Lord and start showing our gratitude?

A Glorious Future is About to Bloom

60 million abortions have been performed under Roe vs. Wade
That's 1.3 million babies every year we've betrayed
They had no voice at all in this decision to end their life
It's murder just as surely as if they were stabbed with a knife

Mass shootings over the last 7 years have totaled 934
From the hysteria, it just seems like there were many more
Not that nothing should be done about these senseless crimes
But for the unborn who were slain, where's the outrage in kind?

Roughly 5 million U.S. soldiers were killed in modern day wars
For sure, their numbers and sacrifice are hard to ignore
But it still pales in comparison to those who never had a chance
To experience all there is to life--to learn, to grow, and advance

Many have rallied around the theme, "Black Lives Matter"
In the news and on the internet, it's created a lot of chatter
There can be no doubt that this catch phrase is certainly true
But shouldn't "Unborn Lives Matter" also be given its due?

Which one might have been the next Newton or Einstein?
Maybe another Lincoln or Martin Luther King we'd find
Which one might have been a player on the world stage
Or won the Nobel Peace Prize before the end of his days?

We'll never know because they never had a chance to speak
It was inconvenient or maybe our values were just too weak
Why do we find it easier to play God and squelch this voice
Rather than accepting responsibility with a much better choice

One of the key issues seems to be when is life's inception?
Is it at birth, at the first heartbeat, or at conception?
The Lord said, "before I formed you in the womb, I knew you"
I think that proclamation leaves little to misconstrue

Some say, when it comes to her body, it's a woman's right
To decide if the fetus she's carrying will ever see the light
No consideration is given to the right of the baby to find his place
To live, to raise a family, or contribute to the human race

When God looks down on how we justify killing the unborn
I believe He reacts with an equal measure of tears and scorn
The time is coming when we'll regret not reaching higher
We'll stand before the throne and face the Lake of Fire

Many women have, after the fact, had second thoughts
As they dealt with the pain, loss, and guilt it brought
Wondering who their child might have turned out to be
And what part he may have played in changing history

I have a personal stake in this drama as do many others
You see my birth was the decision of an unwed mother
She just couldn't bring herself to throw me away
Without her choice, I'd not be writing poetry today

For anyone who might be facing this difficult choice
Listen to your heart and the counsel of your inner voice
That's the Lord speaking for the fetus in your womb
Telling you what a glorious future is about to bloom.

Be a Peter and Step Out of the Boat

Peter was strong in character, ambitious, and outspoken
But he was missing when his Lord's body was beaten and broken
So why did Jesus look around at His followers, take stock
And decide that this flawed disciple would be His rock

It all goes back to his faith being tested on the Galilee, I think
The only one stepping out of the boat, not expecting to sink
Peter would go on to be the leader Christ needed and expected
Emboldened by the Holy Spirit and moved by Jesus resurrected

So what impact does this have on us who proclaim to follow Christ?
What will we do to spread the gospel and at what price?
Are we doing our part to bring people to the streets of gold?
Or are we making excuses—no skills and way too old?

I think, like those twelve, we need a change of mind
And when we do that, here's what I believe we'll find
The tasks He places before us will surely seem small
Compared to the challenges He set before Peter and Paul

We might be a little tentative when we take that first step
But faith will carry us across the water if we just accept
That He is with us each and every step of the way
That His power will calm the storm and all fears allay

We're not going to be martyred like those fishers of men
But I believe He's going to call on us again and again
When the others sit back and wait for the story to be wrote
Don't wait for someone else; be a Peter and step out of the boat.

Black Can Never Be White

When I was a kid the bad guys always wore black
And they always lost to those in white, that's a fact
We cheered on the good guys, knowing they were right
Things might look bad, but they always won the fight

It was a simpler time with very little gray
Completely the opposite of what we have today
The words in the Bible made everything crystal clear
If we did wrong, it was the wrath of God we feared

White is the truth; not determined by the beholder's eyes
And black presents itself as a growing pack of lies
The gray happens when it's a half-truth we buy
Despite how close it is to the truth, it's still a lie

Accepting half-truths is the start down a slippery slope
In short order, finding the truth has lost all hope
The lies build on one another until there's no end
And we accept them like a long lost friend

Look at what's happened to our society today
The lies have become so widespread we've lost our way
Pre-marital sex isn't even given a second thought
And killing babies is a right women have fanatically sought

We don't even know if we're women or men
Or which bathroom we're supposed to attend
And apparently that decision is subject to change
Depending on how our hormones rearrange

The last time the U.S. was debt-free was 1835
The bill today is $15,000 for every person alive
Our politicians lead us to believe we're doing fine
But we all know in our hearts it's just another line.

Thugs are wearing the white hats of individuality
And placing black hats on those in authority
We don't stand for the flag our ancestors died for
Or the ones who are still dying on some distant shore

If we blend black with white, we always get gray
And if we do it long enough, only black will be in play
No matter that some try to convince us this is all right
In our heart, we know black can never be white.

Body, Mind, and Soul

We hear a lot about body, mind, and soul
The three parts of each of us that make us whole
And man has learned much about the first two
But about the third, we're still without a clue

Great strides have been made in how the body works
There's a pill for just about every kind of hurt
Almost every part of the body can be replaced
Medical knowledge advancing at a frenetic pace

Diseases that were once the scourge of society
Have been nearly eliminated from our vocabulary
Even diseases like cancer and those of the heart
Are no longer the death sentence they were at the start

And we seem to be unlocking some mysteries of the brain
Surgeries thought impossible are performed again and again
We're learning how we learn and how we forget
Where our emotions come from—anger, love and regret

We're beginning to see how mind and body work together
To make this living, breathing organism function better
The brain is a very complex computer and overseeing mentor
Body parts respond to the instruction of this control center

But what about that third element, the one we call soul?
Considered to be the center of choice and self-control
Why can't we locate it anywhere in the body physique?
If it's the one thing that makes each of us unique

We know without it, the body stops functioning and dies
Yet, we cannot find where this vital part lies
All of the body parts are still there, but now they don't work
Because what makes us "us" has departed from this earth

This is the one part of us medicine or science cannot explain
And there's good reason why what we know is not germane
It's the spiritual hub that our Creator placed in each of us
And it makes us who we are, in whom or what we put our trust

There are so many things from God not completely understood
But He did promise that there is a day coming when we would
That when we die, He reclaims that part of us we know as soul
And we move on to another dimension of existence, another fold

We can't see our soul just like we can't see heaven
It's one of the mysteries God chooses to keep hidden
But it's our lifeline, the connector between us and Him
If that connector is broken, we're doomed to a life of sin

A church without believers is just a building, dead
But filled with believers, it's very much alive instead
So it is with our bodies, without souls they die
And while on earth, we'll just never understand why

As hard as it may be, the soul is to be honored the most
It's the receptor given to us by our Lord and heavenly host
It's our spiritual lifeline telling us what we should be
And it's our key to a life with Him in eternity

There's a whole spiritual world we just cannot see
But it's more real than the starkest reality
And there's only one connection to it; it's called soul
While not understood, it's what makes us whole.

Butterfly

It all starts inconsequentially with the egg deposited on a leaf
It's such a small beginning it's hardly visible to the naked eye
But what's about to happen is almost beyond belief
It's a transformation that will absolutely amaze and mystify

In short order, this multi-legged creature appears before our eyes
Its voracious appetite devours the leaf it's on and many, many more
It grows rapidly to four or five times its original size
But this caterpillar gives us no hint of the change that's in store

Like us humans after we've eaten too much, the caterpillar rests
He wraps himself up in this blanket which we call a cocoon
We might think there's nothing happening, just a time to digest
But a dramatic change is coming and it's coming soon

The cocoon begins to open and a completely new creature appears
It's nothing at all like the caterpillar; it seems almost like magic
We're not quite sure what to expect as the big moment nears
But the beautiful butterfly emerging is both amazing and dramatic

There's another kind of transformation that will much more astound
The butterfly is a metaphor for how the unbeliever can change
The egg represents just the beginning of a new life found
Just listening passively to the message begins to loosen the chains

The caterpillar represents an intense period of studying God's Word
A voracious appetite develops for understanding everything in the Bible
He learns to listen to instruction coming directly from the Lord
His passion for knowledge of Jesus Christ, the Savior, has no rival

The cocoon stage represents a time of dramatic change and reflection
Connecting the understanding of the mind with acceptance of the heart
Marveling that God would come to earth and save us by resurrection
And we have to do very little---just by accepting His gift, we do our part

The butterfly emerges and spreads its wings like an opening flower
It's a scene that enthralls, full of wonder, a truly spectacular feat
But not nearly as spectacular as the impact of the Holy Spirit's power
The one that indwells and makes the believer's transformation complete

Like the butterfly, this emerging believer is a completely different type
More compassionate, peaceful; it's the Lord he wants to glorify
He's shut out all the worldly din---the distortions, the lies, and the hype
He's been transformed through the blood of Christ; he's a butterfly.

Bollards of Faith

Terrorism just seems to darken our lives every day
Authorities work hard to keep such criminals at bay
Whether it be protecting our planes or our schools
They're challenged to come up with new effective tools

Vehicular bombs have been around for some time
But there's a new form of terror coming on line
Vehicles which are driven off road in a fit of rage
Bowling over anyone who happens to get in the way

One of the means designed to protect from this insanity
Is to erect barriers to prevent this form of brutality
They're called bollards, poles anchored in concrete
Aimed at making this form of terrorism obsolete

In thinking about this, I began to wonder
What kind of risks to our faith are we under
What spiritual bollards have we installed?
How effective are they in resisting Satan's call?

The first bollard I believe is God's Word
The best defense against sin I've ever heard
On its pages are His answers to all situations
Directing each of us on the way to eternal salvation

The second bollard stands firmly next to the first
Its power is strong enough to thwart the most dire curse
It's those Christians who have your back in fellowship
There to hold you accountable, not let your standards slip

A third bollard is your conscience, a kind of guiding light
The go/no go device separating wrong from right
It will go off like a gong if you make a bad choice
But only you will hear this unmistakable inner voice

The fourth bollard is the most important of all
It will bring you back when temptation calls
The strength of this bollard is beyond compare
It's the bollard of reverence and dedicated prayer

There are bollards everywhere protecting you from sin
And God will erect even more if you just tune Him in
So when troubled times hit, stand tall and wait
Secure behind those impenetrable bollards of faith.

Catch 22 Politics

Years ago there was a movie out called Catch 22
A kind of comedic punch at the military in WW II
The Catch is you can get out of the military if you're declared insane
But wanting out proves you have a perfectly normal brain

When I look at our current political situation here at home
Our democracy seems to have developed a Catch 22 of its own
More government freebies must end if we're to be financially OK
But no one gets elected without new things to give away

And so the national debt grows by trillions each year
We take on more debt with seemingly no concerns or fear
But the day is coming when it all comes crashing down
We're on our way to a complete and catastrophic meltdown

So what about this conundrum; what can we do?
How are we to avoid the disaster caused by Catch 22?
How can we stop digging a deeper and deeper hole?
And not elect people to office based on expanding the dole?

Term limits would go a long way to ending this doom
But politicians limiting themselves is not coming anytime soon
Dropping the mindset that I'm entitled and it's all about me
Also doesn't seem likely to end this growing insanity

For decades, this kind of thinking has been going on
A train wreck is coming and it won't be long
Only a complete collapse may set us on the right track
And restore our red balance sheet to the black

It's like God has given us a long rope of free will
A mountain of debt stands where once was a hill
But one day the bill we've generated will come due
And God will end the problem of Catch 22.

Catalina Mountain Moods

I went to the mountains; only emptiness there
Hawks and their buddies had flown south somewhere
Animals along the ground had departed for water and food
And the mountain was engrossed in a somber mood

I went to the mountains; snow-covered its peaks
In the quiet of the moment, nature still speaks
Crisp, clean air permeates my waiting lungs
And my soul is hostage to the glistening sun

I went to the mountains, black as could be
Dark and foreboding robbed my security
Uneasiness settles over that sinister mount
As if some unseen calamity is about to play out

I went to the mountains; nothing could I see
A foggy mist sequesters its ridges in canopy
This ghastly shroud stokes my latent fears
And I'm comforted when it finally clears

I went to the mountains, ominous clouds on high
Lightning, God's laser show, arcs across the sky
Thunder jolts me from my stuporous trance
First raindrops strike the rocks and dance

I went to the mountains, feeling quite low
But my spirit was lifted by a double rainbow
No matter how troublesome or challenging the day
Rainbows are God's promise that all is OK

I went to the mountains, clothed emerald green
Watched plants spring to life and animals preen
Listened carefully and heard the refrain
Of nature's joyous acceptance of monsoon rain

I went to the mountains, golden in drape
Saguaros step out from the desert landscape
Rocks acquire a luster with the evening light
Afternoon's radiant showcase gives way to the night

I went to the mountains, Beethoven there
Hawks and turkey vultures float on a carpet of air
It's nature's symphony played out before our eyes
As they dip below the horizon, then catch a thermal and rise

I went to the mountains, clouds all apuff
Fill my senses with their winsome fluff
They hang there on the cliffs, attached it seems
It's a magical time and it fuels my dreams

I went to the mountains in the darkness of night
A silhouette against the sky, reflecting power and might
A billion stars captivate the setting as only they can
A full moon perches on the ridge, as if placed there by hand

I go to the mountains, sometimes only in mind
As I extend my gaze upward, here's what I find
Each interlude is different, always mesmerizing and new
And I say "thank you Lord for this magnificent view".

Circle of Life

Just separate pieces of the puzzle, body and soul
Till God joins them together to make one whole
And a unique person is created at this moment in time
Even though the birth itself is further down the line

The writhing, squirming infant emerges from the womb
The proud father cheering the arrival from across the room
This completely helpless one can do nothing on his own
But does add to the happiness quotient of this loving home

Baby followed on by toddler, inquisitiveness beyond compare
If you don't want your "pretty" broken, better not leave it there
It's that time to explore everything that's within the grasp
Only recently learned to walk, but still gets there fast

The pre-teen years, a period of rapid learning and growth
Still leaning heavily on mom and dad; needing them both
Virtually no awareness of the soul through this time
A happy period, simple concerns, the world looks fine

The teen period, a time of change, see what unfurls
Emotions, raging hormones and yes, first awareness of girls
Discovery, peer pressure, and depression all rolled into one
Awareness of the soul is there but only barely begun

Young adulthood brings with it new challenges and fears
Which route, college or a trade on which to build a career?
Beginning to once again understand how little we know
And God keeps strengthening that thing called soul

Then she comes and life's never quite the same
There's nothing she wouldn't do, even change her name
We're standing at the altar, her hand in mine
What lies ahead will only be told by the passage of time

It's not long before beautiful children come along
There's pressure but it gives in to joy; life's a song
The years pass so quickly we can hardly believe
They're all grown up---adults themselves and ready to leave

And all this time God's Spirit speaks as never before
There's push back but it's a voice that can't be ignored
That thing he placed inside, what we call soul
Makes us this unique individual, that we know

The autumn of our years has finally arrived
We're thankful for each day given; each day alive
We're concerned with the body, but much more with the soul
Our focus on the spiritual intensifies as we grow old

Once more we are dependent, childlike, a wretch
Simple tasks we once took for granted are now a stretch
We need help walking, eating; understanding's a chore
Hair is thinning and fading is our memory of all things before

Our body and soul, once joined are separated again
The body goes to ashes; the soul to Him
And with this soul crossing to the other side
We complete the circle of life to be by His side.

Complete Trust

In life, there are so many things where trust is a given
Someone or something we count on as part of livin'
We believe that the plane we're in will not come down
Or that other drivers will not run the red lights in town

We trust that the bank will not steal our money
That the rain will give way to days that are sunny
That the cruise ship we're on will not sink
And that we'll be all right if we trust our instincts

The running back trusts his linemen to open a hole
And the basketball player relies on the pick and roll
When the game's on the line, the team trusts its star
Because he's the one who brought them this far

We place our money in a trust for the next generation
To give them a future with a solid foundation
By working hard, we trust we'll stay employed
And continue the lifestyle that we've so enjoyed

There is some measure of trust wherever we turn
From child to adult it's something we learn
In its absence, we're nothing but a chaotic society
Living in fear and distrust, paralyzed by anxiety

But when it comes to God, the notion seems like a crutch
Even though our currency says "In God We Trust"
When times are good, we rely on our own control
But in tough times, there are no atheists in the foxhole

I think we act like this because we don't truly believe
That God's awesome power created everything we see
That He is concerned about our life, every detail
That He is with us every day, every hour without fail

I have to admit there are times when I put my trust in me
And my short-term view of how things should be
My limitations are evident, I just can't comprehend
How I can follow the unknowns of God's perfect plan

So I go my own way; I'm so much a work in progress
But I know deep in my heart that I'll never have success
Until I set aside my own free will, listen, and adjust
Placing all my confidence in the only One I can trust

If I can just do that, I know I'll spend eternity with Him
Even though my life is one of disobedience and sin
It's been a long-time coming, but I'm learning it's a must
That only in Him and His grace can I have complete trust.

Contrails

The other day I noticed several jets moving across the blue
Wending their way, they left a contrail as they flew
The fast-moving planes disappeared before too long
But their contrails lingered awhile before they were gone

It got me to wondering what contrails do we leave?
What stories about us will succeeding generations believe?
Will there be wonderful memories for them to recall?
Or when you're gone, will there be no contrail at all?

Will there be anything for your grandchildren to see?
Or will your story not even qualify as a fading memory?
Will they listen to tales about great grandpa with glee?
Or will there be just empty pages for your legacy?

There's an old country song I've sung a few times
About leaving this world and what you leave behind
It's not what you take when you leave you know
It's what you leave behind you when you go

So what are my options; what can I, an old man, really do
There's no paucity of choices, so let me give you a few
Make memories now that your family will never forget
Those contrails with staying power that linger after the jet

Produce a video, organize those photographs, write a book
Do something wild and crazy; an adventure undertook
It's the out-of-character moments, not the blasé
That people will remember long past your day

Set an example for the children to emulate and live by
Show them there's a time for laughter and a time to cry
That challenge brings growth and the good guy wins
And that regardless of what life brings, you can trust in Him

That truth and integrity will never make the nightly news
But will bring friendships and relationships you'll never lose
And during those times when your life seems in tatters
It's the love of those closest to you that really matters

We have no idea how long we'll have till God reclaims our soul
Because when all is said and done, it's He who's in control
Just remember, when life jets by and your person is out of view
It's your contrail that will determine how they'll remember you.

Contemplating the Lord's Prayer

Our Father
Not our physical father, but our spiritual one
The one who so loved us He sacrificed His only Son

Who art in Heaven
Heaven is where the God of the Universe resides
But even on earth He is always by our side

Hallowed be thy name
His name is above all others since the beginning of time
His name is the one which should fill our hearts and minds

Thy kingdom come
His kingdom will reign and it will have no end
His enemies will all be vanquished; every knee will bend

Thy will be done on earth as it is in heaven
In heaven and on earth God will have his way
And we would do well to follow His will every day

Give us this day our daily bread
Everything we have or will have God provides
Each day is a gift from our Lord Most High

And forgive our trespasses as we forgive those who trespass against us
As God forgives us, we must forgive others
We are all children of God; we're all brothers

And lead us not into temptation
We are in a battle between the spirit and the flesh
Give us discernment and strength to choose best

But deliver us from evil
Protect us from the evil one and his many schemes
His is the easy path, but it's not what it seems

For thine is the kingdom and the power and the glory forever
One day each of us must approach the throne
And acknowledge that He is Lord of all, He alone

Amen
You can believe it
So be it.

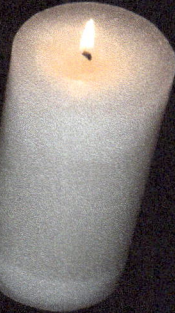

Corona

Corona, corona, what have you done?
Disrupted our lives and curtailed our fun
When will your long tentacles release their grip?
When will peace appear and joy return to our lips?

You've taken over our lives, every facet of our day
You've brought out the worst of us in every way
We fight over toilet paper, sanitizer, and soap
A once optimistic nation seems to have lost all hope

A new vocabulary and strange thoughts have spawned
Social distancing and self-quarantine have entered our lexicon
Talk centers on hazmat suits, ventilators, and shelter in place
Wash your hands for 20 seconds, but don't touch your face

401K's have tanked and riding-high stocks have bit the dust
There's no kind of investment that hasn't gone bust
Health care workers and others in service risk it all
Modern-day heroes who have willingly answered the call

Shuttered stadia, theaters, churches, and restaurants
Curb-side is all that's available from your local haunt
People out of work and devastating shutdowns everywhere
We're tempted to ask "God, are you still up there?"

Corona, you may think you're the victor on this wild ride
But when I look around I see quite another side
People are helping other people where they see a need
They're coming together not only in thought, but in deed

Shopping for a neighbor as part of our trip to the store
Sending over a meal to someone we hardly knew before
Families across the country checking in by phone
Touching base with someone who may be feeling alone

Companies setting aside the profit motive for just awhile
Treating their employees with a measure of grace and style
People admitting they might actually need prayer
Our government really doing something to relieve despair

With all facilities closed, people are walking for recreation
Maybe for the first time taking in the beauty of God's creation
We're in the habit of running here and there 100% of the time
But I see us rediscovering the walk as a way to unwind

God did not bring this virus upon us but He's putting it to use
We're not meant to live with our gadgets as a kind of recluse
We're a social animal; we must work, play and live together
And when we support each other, we're so much better

God is showing us what a great place this earth can be
If we just help our neighbor and discard "It's all about me"
So what do you say we get started and when corona ends
We open our hearts and with love, live the way God intends?

Crimson Clouds and Sliver Moon

The world has a lot of ugly that's for sure
Shootings, cancer, crime, and so much more
It's on TV, on the social media, and in the news
There's not much wholesomeness we can choose

Our once-beautiful countryside is often a dumping ground
Graffiti seems to adorn every empty wall in town
Our oceans and beaches are awash with what we throw away
Smokers treat the earth as one massive ash tray

And yet, if we close down the ugly, there is beauty all around
It's a gift from God to pick us up when we're down
The ugly disappears if we but focus on nature for just awhile
It will lift your spirits, change your attitude, and make you smile

There are the flowers of Spring, glorious colors abound
The blossoms of cherry and apple gently snowing down
Our senses take great pleasure, both sight and smell
And in the process, soothe our longing soul as well

There's the emerald green grass our feet caress
The soft breeze through the forest that kills our stress
The fresh blanket of snow that moved in overnight
Making the first tracks through the carpet of white

There's that peaceful stroll on the deserted beach
Where all of God's wondrous creation is within reach
The waves pound into the shore and crash on the rocks
Sailboats slip home for the evening and line the docks

The roar of the thunder and the flash close behind
The plants that stretch up with the water they find
And when the storm is over and quiet resumes
There's the rainbow bouquet over all that looms

But there's nothing quite comparable to a golden sunset
The clouds streak with crimson in a way you can't forget
And when the setting sun brings closure to the afternoon
We can imagine ourself quietly swinging on a sliver moon

God never intended we would lead a life of stress
And His presentation of nature is peace at its best
So when you're about to roll up in a tight cocoon
Recall the beauty of the crimson clouds and sliver moon.

Dichotomy of Our Times

Our buildings are taller, but our tempers so short
Our freeways are wider, but narrower our views
We've lost the sense of family, but found the courts
We have a pill for everything, but still suffer the blues

We spend more on material, but in spirit, have less
We have more conveniences, but are short on time
We are quick to accuse, but slow on forgiveness
We're connected to the church, but not to the vine

We have GPS, but we've still lost our way
We talk too much and don't listen enough
We watch TV too much, but only in crisis, pray
We have God-given gifts, but easily give up

We support our freedoms, but not the price of defense
Our houses are bigger, but we haven't learned how to live
We have multiple degrees, but no common sense
We're so much better at "take" than we are at "give"

We treasure getting ahead, but don't want to labor
We're cleaning up the air, but polluting our soul
We've been to the moon, but do we know our neighbor?
We make more money, but find it difficult to stay whole

It's the age of instant everything, including divorce
We know there's no need to rush, but we just can't wait
We have less real love, but more meaningless intercourse
We demand medical miracles, but we're overweight

We've learned to make a living, but our life's a waste
We want a cleaner environment, but trash our roads
We've conquered outer space, but not inner space
And we don't expect to reap whatever we've sowed

There's much in the showroom, but nothing in the stockroom
We communicate expertly on our devices, but fumble face to face
Big men with small character make us dance to their tune
Technology races forward, but we need to slow down the pace

The dichotomy of our lives has never been more evident
We talk the talk, but our actual walk falls behind
When will our values and actions become congruent?
Our heart continues to wrestle with what's on our mind

I think God is disappointed in our blatant hypocrisy
Only through Him can we both see and live the truth
And maybe acknowledge it's not all about me
By making a real effort to pray to our Lord and improve

It's not that complicated, folks, to get our act together
Lining up our values with what we say and do
Jesus showed us in a short 33 years how to be better
It can be done one person at a time; it's up to me and you.

Distractions

Life is full of distractions of all kinds
And they can quickly divert whatever's on our mind
That is especially true of the world we live in today
It is increasingly difficult to keep such diversions at bay

Sometimes I look back at the world of my childhood
Simple, quiet, focused, even boring, but good
We played board games and chatted over a meal
Evening swings on the front porch were a big deal

People dropped by unannounced and it was OK
The kids were probably out playing ball all day
And we were able to focus on the task at hand
Life felt unhurried and we listened to the Man

But today we just seem to be in hurry-up mode
And there is just precious little to lighten our load
It feels like we're in a race and we're falling behind
Where's the peace we so desperately want to find?

A large part of our frustration comes from technology
Messages bombard us every day on the internet and TV
We can't resist, wherever we are, the call of the I-Phone
Downtime is almost non-existent; we're never alone

There's a lot of talk today about ADD or lack of attention span
And there's much about this disorder I don't understand
But I do know the society we live in makes the problem worse
And the distractions all around us are a modern-day curse

So what are we to do to find our own Golden Pond?
How do we set all the distractions aside and bond?
How do we begin recovering that sense of family fun?
Actually talking to each other without moving our thumbs

I'm not suggesting we have to give the wonders of technology up
But we have to find ways to step out of this digital rut
We need a time period when we shut all the interruptions down
Talk to each other and to the Lord with no distracting sound

You'll not be able to hear Him above the worldly noise
Make a daily appointment with Him; it's simply a choice.
Make finding your quiet place a part of each and every day
Where it's quiet and you can hear what the Lord has to say.

EGR

Someone cuts you off on the interstate
Or blows their horn because they just can't wait
Or gives you the high sign from their car
You don't react because you know about EGR

Someone cuts in front of you in the ticket line
You'd really like to give them a piece of your mind
But you hold back, not choosing the verbal spar
You recognize they're just someone in need of EGR

You meet someone who regales about his multiple degrees
And how this knowledge helped him become a corporate VP
The implication being you fell short in not getting that far
Time to tone down your feelings and bring out the EGR

There's the one who likes to dominate every conversation
On any subject, he can pontificate without cessation
In every gathering, he's the unquestionable star
And in need of a large helping of EGR

There's the guy at the party with no social graces
Saying all the wrong things in all the wrong places
May have made too many trips to the wine bar
Loud and obnoxious, he needs mega-doses of EGR

We all know those who, if put in charge, could do it better
But we know them as just commentators, not go-getters
Not the kind to roll up their sleeves; that's not who they are
But we're obligated to show them love through EGR

Four of us go out to dinner, but when the check comes around
Those friends with alligator arms just can't be found
They're not French, but they've gone "au revoir"
We dish out not only the money, but the EGR

Some just go through life high on the "grumpy scale"
They see the negative side of everything without fail
I have to admit I'm one who often sees the half-empty jar
I'm so glad my wife and friends offer plenty of EGR

We encounter EGR people every day in our travels
At times, our patience comes nearly unraveled
But then, the Lord speaks and we are inspired
To give a pass to those of EXTRA GRACE REQUIRED.

Enough

Blessed beyond what we can describe
Sufficiency evident, if conscience be our guide
So not wishing you more irrelevant stuff
What I wish for you is I wish you enough

Enough cloudy, dreary, and rainy days
That you revel in the sun and bask in its rays
Enough failure in business and other relations
That success in either brings wild elation

Enough ache in your step that when the hurt's done
You cherish the moment you can freely run
Enough affliction in your day-to-day livin'
That good health is not viewed as a given

Enough wonder at the nighttime universe
That you believe God's Word, chapter and verse
Enough adult decisions, made and filed
That you delight in showing your inner child

Enough scars from skirmishes that never cease
That you can truly celebrate a lasting peace
Enough love lost in the dating run
That you recognize and idolize "The One"

Enough grind-and-sweat labor every day
That you can devote the same energy to when you play
Enough enemies, real or perceived
That investing in friendships is what you believe

Enough fear and trepidation in all things new
That you accomplish more than you thought you could do
Enough cold, lonely, and sleepless nights
That you can take "warm and cuddly" to new heights

Victory is much sweeter after a resounding defeat
Love found after love lost is hard to beat
That's why some challenge is good; times that are tough
And why my wish for you is I wish you enough.

Find Your Puddle

I'm always intrigued how a dog reacts to a puddle
You can bet his actions are anything but subtle
Most likely he'll go prancing through the little lake
Exiting all wet and frisky, make no mistake

Whereas people would just stop and walk around
The dog runs through the middle in a few bounds
He just seems to find so much joy in this little escapade
Romping in sheer delight, a new game to be played

Kids will react to a puddle in much the same way
Boots or not, the puddle is an invitation to play
And the joy they find is written all over their faces
Giggling and splashing through the deepest places

So what puddles do we have that wildly exhilarate?
What elevates our joy and raises our heart rate?
What makes us forget our troubles for just a bit
Or makes us laugh till we just can't quit?

Maybe your puddle is the adrenalin of a skydiving trip
Or the adventure of crewing a sailing ship
Maybe it's a dive to the darkest depths of the sea
Or the beauty of a cruise through the isles of Hawaii

Maybe it's a hike down the Grand Canyon one time
Or a dinner cruise down the River Rhine
Maybe it's joining your kids on the slip-and-slide
Something bringing joy you just can't hide

Maybe it's a trip to Africa you thought could never be
Seeing the animals up close, roaming wild and free
Or building a snowman together after a heavy snow
Or whisking down a scary zip line in old Mexico

Jesus said "I come that you would have life to the full"
Our lives were never meant to be just a daily struggle
Joy in heaven-yes, but we also need it on earth
Each day we should be living it for all it's worth

There's a puddle out there, just waiting for you
It's a puddle that only you can run through
Life is too short to have it be just a muddle
But it's up to you to find your puddle.

Fly Like an Eagle

Eagles are clearly one of our most majestic birds
Their maneuvers in the sky astound beyond words
Despite their awesome wingspan and impressive size
No wing movement is needed to dramatically fall or rise

They've learned to dance on the air like a Baryshnikov ballet
It could be put to music, this phenomenal display
They wing their way through the blue with no effort at all
It's as smooth as a Viennese waltz at a gala ball

Eagles always nest in high places, either cliffs or trees
But how do the eaglets acquire this soaring expertise?
How do they discover the elegance when it's their turn?
And what are the baby steps it takes to learn?

It's a lot like a baby venturing out to take his first steps
It involves a very short distance and many, many reps
The eaglet will hop from branch to branch with wings aflap
Then short flights to more distant branches and back

Then finally with wings fully extended, it's a leap of faith
And he's off to the wind to meet destiny's fate
He is obligated to leave the security of his parents' nest
And set out on his own adventure, his personal quest

He still has to learn the intricacies of managing the thermals
Floating on the updrafts until it's second nature and normal
Doing and being everything God imagined him to be
And setting a standard of beauty and unequaled majesty

Isn't this a great analogy for what God expects of us?
Our days were never intended to be quite superfluous
We're not meant to spend our lifetime in our comfort zone
Instead we must spread our wings and strike out on our own

Like the eaglet, it may take a number of small beginnings
Until we feel secure to take on the world and spread our wings
Until we can learn how to master the downs and enjoy the lifts
Appreciating what life has to offer and accepting the gifts

So the next time you see an eagle floating on the air
Imagine how wonderful life could be with you up there
You may be poor but your days can still be regal
If you just spread your wings and fly like an eagle.

Follow the Light

Where do we go today when we want answers to almost anything?
Don't we just fire up our computer and consult with the Google king?
Early man didn't have the benefit of the I-Pad or the I-Phone
But he understood so much more completely we're not alone

He knew that God provided the answers if we just looked to the sky
The timeless questions of the meaning of life—the who, what, and why
From the very beginning, man knew that evil lurked in the dark
But also knew that God could shine a light into each man's heart

On the first day of Creation, God said let there be light and there was
It was called day when light prevails and night when darkness does
The sun provided all that was needed, warmth and comfort each day
But it was in the darkness that we stumbled and lost our way

God sent the sun but He also sent His Son to light our path
Jesus obeyed his Father's will and took the punishment on our behalf
His light shines brighter than any sun or any cavalcade of stars
And it's only through Him we discover why we're here and who we are

Let's be clear, there's a lot of darkness everywhere we look
And the answers are not going to be found in some self-help book
But if you just follow Jesus' example, you'll be doing all right
The answers are there; look to the heavens and follow the light.

Footprints on My Heart

Almost everyone knows the "Footprints in the Sand" poem
Showing us that in troubled times we are not alone
That we can handle it all when things are stable
But He carries us when we we're weak and unable

There are two sets of footprints when times are fun
But when trouble develops, there seems to be only one
This is a great analogy that I wouldn't want to dismiss
But I think there's at least one other way to look at this

Most of the time I noticed there were two sets of prints
God and I walking together; that made sense
But occasionally there was only one set of tracks evident
Times when I no longer wanted or needed His consent

My tracks wandered off and were quickly washed away
But God's were there waiting for me to return to His way
And when I did He completely forgave my excursion
Took my hand again and we walked off my every burden

You would think I'd have learned my lesson, but I wander still
It's a gift that God gave all of us and it's called free will
He wants us to walk with Him, but it's still our choice
He speaks quietly and we must listen intently to hear His voice

One day I hope our footprints will run for miles side by side
That we will always walk together and I'll have nothing to hide
That every day of my life God and I will never be apart
And His footprints will not only be in the sand, but on my heart.

Footsteps of Dorian Gray

You may recall the book, "A Picture of Dorian Gray"
Oscar Wilde created quite a stir with it in his day
It's about a handsome young man who's all the rage
Despite his advancing years, he just never seems to age

But a painting of him at home tells quite a different tale
The painting picks up all the signs of aging in great detail
Every act of debauchery is recorded right there on his face
While the mask he wears in real life conceals his disgrace

For every sin he commits, the painting develops new wrinkles
New signs of aging appear—scars, moles, and pimples
The painting becomes decrepit---bald and tired, with sagging skin
While Dorian keeps his childish good looks and winsome grin

John Wooden once said, "Reputation is what people think you are"
And on that alone, some may elevate you to the class of superstar
But he defined character as what you really are, as seen by God
You could present a great face to the world and it be just a facade

Of course, none of us have a painting in the attic like Dorian Gray
But God has such a painting that makes Him sad every day
He wants so much for our painting and our real self to be the same
A heart that's pure, a mind that's clean, and a soul absent of shame

He knew that, on our own, we could never be reconciled to Him
That only by sending His Son could death be brought to sin
So that when Christ intercedes for us on Judgment Day
Our painting and our real self will the same picture display

So, I pray you're not a double agent in the way you lead your life
That who you are in public and when no one's watching are just alike
That you're becoming more like Christ each and every day
And not following in the misguided footsteps of Dorian Gray.

Ford Fairlanes in a Tesla World

We find it's time to replace that old car with one shiny and new
One where everything works just the way it's supposed to
Then the years go by and gradually the car falls apart
Its advances no longer excite us like they did at the start

Hoses carrying various fluids have a tendency to leak
The parts that were once quiet now begin to squeak
That once spotless finish is decorated with scratches and dents
And we can't help but wonder where 0 to 60 went

Those with new-technology cars smile as they hurry by
And all we can do is manage a look of envy and sigh
The car that used to impress now more often just stops
And we look for a tow to the nearest repair shop

But some of these cars seemingly ready for final scrap
Find a second life and a way to set the clock back
Someone with the necessary skills restores its original lure
And that wreck becomes a classic that turns heads for sure

Isn't this car saga a lot like us as we walk life's beat?
In youth, there's seemingly no challenge we can't meet
We're beautiful, strong, articulate, and fast
And we think that everything we are will forever last

But time, worry, and wear and tear take their toll
One day we look in the mirror and discover we're old
Proof lies in the replacement parts for knees and hips
The hearing loss, sagging skin and how our memory slips

We can no longer compete with the skills of the younger set
Their capacity for memory is outdone by ours to forget
These losses affect us equally, whether boy or girl
We find we're just Ford Fairlanes in a Tesla world

But in this dismal situation, restoration can still be achieved
God promised perfect bodies again for those who believe
Like that Ford Fairlane, we can be restored to our former glory
The salvage-yard cemetery will not be the end of our story

It will look like a classic car show when we're at the throne
This collection of saints, shining like the world has never known
Our engines will be purring like we were never old
And we'll be racing each other down those streets of gold

And in the meantime, those Teslas will succumb to the latest fad
They'll be replaced by the new model everyone wishes they had
And for us, when life no longer resembles a stroll through the clover
God will be there to provide us with the ultimate makeover.

Forever Dad

I was there when you made your earthly debut
Cradling you in my arms before you even knew
That I would be the biggest supporter you ever had
No more special day than when I became your dad

Together I set out on this journey called life with you
Lots of smooth sailing, but some potholes too
Sometimes a road less traveled, but always one of love
Always trying to take guidance from the One above

There have been times when it was less than a perfect plan
In the autumn of my years now, I think back whenever I can
Those childhood memories when we laughed and played
Watching you grow to be an adult and finding your way

I'm sure you thought I was demanding of you at times
But if I was, it was only the best for you I had in mind
Life is a learning curve and sometimes quite a mess
Through it all, I only wanted more for you, never less

I never made the rank of perfect dad, to that I can attest
But you should know I was always giving it my very best
Whenever you needed a helping hand, I believe I was there
Financially and emotionally, stepping up to prove I care

There is nothing you can do that will ever turn me away
I'm afraid you're stuck with me till my dying day
Whatever challenges come your way, I hope you see
That I'm here to help you be the best "you" you can be.

Friend

There when you need them, through thick and thin
Soothing when you lose; celebratory when you win
Standing beside you when it's difficult to cope
Through life's darkest days, bringing hope

Happy to spend time together, doing absolutely nothing
Even the smallest occasion turns into something
Secrets shared that will never be heard
Help that comes without even a word

Accepting all our idiosyncrasies and quirks
Rolling up their sleeves when it's time to work
When others talk about you in rumor and lie
They don't participate or even ask why

You have a lot in common; interests you share
In times of trouble, you're in their prayers
Not judgmental or convicting in any way
Much like Jesus modeled for us in his day

They know all your weaknesses and yet you're brothers
Lauding your strengths in front of others
Blind to your limitations, just cannot see
That you're half the person they think you to be

They double your joy; cut your sorrow in half
Spontaneous and raucous when sharing a laugh
They know everything about you, but it's OK
Because nothing you do will drive them away

They're life's treasures, that's for sure
Warming our hearts down to the core
Enriching our lives right to the end
That's why we're blessed to call them 'friend'.

God Doesn't Grade On a Curve

It all starts when we're very young
Comparing ourselves to others in what we've done
Our good is better than someone else's good
And our bad is not as bad, just misunderstood

The professor gives us a grade on a college exam of 22
We realize in horror it's an "F"; nothing we can do
We anguish, but then mercifully he posts the curve
We're elevated to a "B", completely undeserved

Likewise, it follows on in our business career
We sweat it out with the layoff announcement near
But the manager has ranked us from one to ten
And by the grace of his "curve" we're safe once again

And so it goes in every facet of life on earth
We don't receive the grade that reflects our worth
With the bear chasing, we don't have to have the fleetest of feet
It's only the slowest of foot that we have to beat

But when it comes to who goes to heaven, it's a different game
It won't matter if we're better, worse, or just the same
We'll stand before the Father and our record He'll observe
Normal probability won't matter; there are no points in reserve

God's standard is perfection, nothing short of 100%
And on our own, there's no chance of that standard being met
It's only through Jesus Christ we get the grade we don't deserve
He's the only way because God doesn't grade on a curve.

God's Finish Line

If you were a marathon runner I think you'll relate
Even if your success was a tad short of great
Learnings from that experience are still applicable today
In responding to life's challenges thrown your way

First and foremost, in running you must have a plan
You can't sprint the whole way even if you think you can
You must conserve energy for the inevitable hills
And save a kick for the end when you're short on will

In every race ever run, your body at some point wants to quit
Bring an end to the pain, give it up, and be done with it
But there's a voice inside that tells you to press on
Just take a few more strides and the victory can be won

I think there's an analogy here about our run for Christ
What are we willing to give up, what to sacrifice?
When the body is weak, will the spirit overcome?
Will we be able to kick it in and finish the run?

The difference between the distance runner and life's grind
Is that, in life, we cannot see how far it is to the finish line
How can we be assured that we've run our best race
If we don't know the distance and don't set the right pace

But then comes the Helper who's always by our side
The Invisible One in whom we can trust and truly confide
The Holy Spirit is there to share with us God's plan
Bringing the example of Jesus to every woman and man

Like the distance runner we're to be in it for the long haul
Running the race God set out for us, pleasing Him above all
We will stumble at times, when rough road comes into play
But Jesus will be waiting with open arms at the end of our days

We will tire and every muscle in our body will tell us to quit
But then we think about the cross and we'll have none of it
Like the runner we push on, persevering over body and mind
And finally, in glory, stretch out over God's finish line.

Free

What does it mean to be truly free?
Here's a picture that may explain it adequately
Let go of your dog's leash with the gate open wide
In a few seconds, he'll vanish from your side

He's running free to somewhere he's never been
You don't know if he'll come back or when
His ears are flopping and he's off to parts unknown
And only when he's hungry, will he return home

Remember the end of the school year, summer vacation?
Running from the building in total celebration
Or when you finally graduated to life's next phase
Throwing your cap in the air in freedom's craze

How about that day when you could finally drive?
Out on the road, feeling blessed just to be alive
It's a sense of freedom like none other, unsurpassed
A sense of controlling your own destiny at last

Then there's the freedom of retirement come due
When you can finally discover the hidden you
When Monday mornings never again matter
And talk of deadlines is just so much chatter

Ask someone who's lived in a totalitarian regime
If freedom doesn't qualify as a blessed dream
Ask them what they'd give up to be totally free
And you'll find no limits to the value of liberty

Many of our soldiers paid an unbelievable price
Most of us cannot imagine the extent of their sacrifice
They risked their life without hesitation or thought
And the world is envious of the freedom they bought

But these freedoms pale in comparison to this one
The day you accepted Jesus as God's only Son
When you felt like you really were born again
Freeing you forever from the power of sin

It's the day you finally knew meaning or truth
It was not the answer to what but the answer to who
Jesus said the way, the truth, and the life is me
You will know the truth and the truth will set you free

And that my friends is the greatest freedom of all
Placing your trust in the Lord when you hear Him call
You'll feel like someone gave you the Fort Knox key
And you'll know for the first time the true meaning of free.

God-man or Goo-man?

Are we the result of a random series of events or made by God?
Is it to Darwin's theory of evolution or to creation we give the nod?
Do we really believe we're descended from the amoeba or paramecium?
Or do we owe everything to the Creator and his risen Son?

Did God breathe life into Adam, as the Bible says, on dry land?
Or did we simply emerge from the swamp as a kind of goo-man?
How do we answer the difficult questions of life for you and I?
Who am I, why am I here, and what happens to me when I die?

If it was 70 fallen leaves all in a perfect row you were seeing
Would you attribute it to happenstance or an intelligent being?
So why do we continue to doubt what's written in the Good Book?
The answers are all there, including creation, if we just look

If you doubt there being a Creator, suggest you look to the sky
Embrace it like a child who stares at it in wonder and wide-eye
Why is there such order to every body in the universe that we see?
How can a computer identify, at any point in time, where each will be?

How can we even fathom forever or conceptual infinity?
When we can't even reach the limits of our own galaxy?
That there are a billion more is just beyond imagination
And yet somehow we cannot embrace the thought of creation

There's the human body, an amazing machine of such complexity
That, at the cellular level, we see astounding order and biochemistry
Mechanisms at work so intriguing they take away our breath
Why is it when we cut our finger, we don't we bleed to death?

So, whether we look outward or inward, the conclusion's the same
He's the Almighty, the Creator, the name to place above all names
It's to Him we are to render all obedience, devotion, and trust
His Commandments are not just a good idea; they're a must

Why is it that man keeps looking in the box for philosophical clues?
And tries to generalize the particulars to a universal worldview
When the universals are all right there for us to read and understand
If we just accept that God sits outside the box, with our fate in His hand

The Bible says God created, in His own image, mankind
Do you think it was a random goo-man He had in mind?
Is it all about us, as Maslow would say, that we self-actualize
Or should we be concerned about how we look in the Creator's eyes?

God showed us in the Garden, He is a jealous god, El Qanna
He expects that we will worship Him in reverence and awe
Not put Him in the box and decide to go our own way
As our secular society seems determined to do today

So what's it going to be? Are we going to bow down to The One?
And give all to the Father, the Holy Spirit, and the Son
Or are we going to believe what's in the box, proven a sham
I don't know about you, but I'm not betting my eternity on the goo-man.

God's Got This

Life is full of challenges and the answers can be few
Experts are everywhere, delighted to tell us what to do
And we like to think for every problem a solution exists
The popular response today being "I got this"

Another popular mantra is the phrase git 'er done
Implying it's all up to us; we don't need anyone
It's a bit like a fairy tale and about as fictitious
When we strut our stuff and proclaim, "I got this"

But we were not created to go it on our own
Despite the bravado for which our culture is known
Sometimes we cannot find the strength within our self
It takes another source from whence comes our help

Often there are people we know offering a helping hand
And it won't diminish our worth or disrupt our plan
If we just accept their help and work together
To lessen the burden and make the outcome better

But sometimes the obstacle we face is more mountain than hill
It just overwhelms our ability and destroys our will
In times like this, there's someone we can trust
Seeking Him in prayer more than a good idea, it's a must

God is there for us every day, every minute and every hour
We can come to Him and tap into his awesome power
Regardless of the situation, small problem or big crisis
We can turn to Him and be assured, "He's got this"

He knows every hair on our head, every thought, every mistake
He's there in the good times and through the heartache
When you've exhausted all options despite intense analysis
Take it up with the Lord because you know "God's got this".

Gone

I awoke one morning and you weren't around
Called your name, but you were not to be found
Asked if you had been seen by any of our friends
And searched for clues for days on end

It took awhile till I realized you'd never return
In the pit of my stomach, something started to churn
Thirty years we'd been together this very year
Yet, in the blink of an eye, you were gone, my dear

As the time passed, I thought of all I'd left unsaid
How petty it seemed now in my hour of dread
Why hadn't I told you you're the lady of my life
And that it was wonderful, you being my wife

That I thought it was great you let me be king
While, behind the scenes, you managed everything
That you were the strength I drew from each day
That I relied on you to show me the way

That I watched in awe how you dealt with others
Shared the joys of the child; the struggles of mothers
Always around with that special touch
The one you can't teach, but means so much.

So why hadn't I told you what was in my heart?
That I needed you every day, right from the start
That you made everything in my life so much better
Why hadn't I written it to you in a love letter?

So if you have something to say to the one you love
Don't let it be just something you're thinking of
Life is unpredictable, stuff happens, and before too long
That special someone who needed those words may be gone.

Good and Faithful Servant – Well Done

He came into the world in the usual way
But was forced to lay His head on a blanket of hay
Only a select few knew this was the King
Or that one day He'd be the Master of everything

His childhood was no indication of what was to come
Or what impact He'd have when His work was done
He challenged the establishment right from the start
Spoke with authority words directly from the heart

12 ordinary men became His followers, his band
Carrying a message even they didn't understand
He was a peasant, humble, but committed to his course
His power just seemed to come from a different source

His followers grew in number each and every day
The establishment became very concerned about the Way
Time and time again they failed to prove Him a fraud
This man might be as He claimed, The Son of God

He was a threat to all the power they held dear
They had to eliminate him that much was clear
Trumped up charges were at the heart of this scam
They just didn't know they were part of His plan

But, with a mob mentality, they sent Him to the cross
Even His most ardent followers thought His life a loss
He seemed ordinary when He called to His Father out loud
When the atonement was complete and His head was bowed

But the hope was rekindled when He arose from the grave
And they knew it was only through Him they could be saved
That eternity wasn't just a nice thought to sugar coat death
That the last air on earth wasn't to be their last breath

The Holy Spirit Jesus had promised came at Pentecost
And ordinary men proclaimed His message at extreme cost
All suffered incredible punishment and most died a horrible death
Yet they stood by their Lord and Savior till their last breath

Most of us will not suffer this kind of anguish in our testimony
But we will be challenged with persecution and acrimony
Like the 12, when that happens we must stand tall
Keeping Christ in view and following the example of Paul

And when our work here on earth has come to an end
And it is time for us to follow our Lord; to heaven ascend
I pray that He would be there to start us on our eternal run
With this greeting, "Oh, good and faithful servant, well done!"

Growth is Fueled By a Lifetime of Mistakes

When we look back, it's easy to see we all made mistakes
But unlike Hollywood, it's usually impossible to do retakes
And all of them come with a measure of sorrow and regret
It can become difficult to move on, to change, and forget

In those cases where we can correct what we did wrong
It behooves us to make restitution, not waiting too long
The path to forgiveness may be difficult, but it cleanses the soul
It will quiet that voice you can't seem to control

I think mistakes are a vital part of God's learning curve
How we move from narcissism to a willingness to serve
The God of the Universe gave us the perfect blueprint
Following the example provided through the Son He sent

God is the master potter and we are are just the clay
He molds and makes us according to His will every day
Sometimes our clay is so bad He has to scrap the whole jar
Remaking what we're called to do and who we are

Lest we think our shortcomings are somehow unique
Even icons of the Bible had moments they were weak
Disobedience kept Moses from entering the Promised Land
And David let his attraction to Bathsheba get out of hand

Mistakes often lead to suffering and being unable to cope
But the Bible says suffering leads to character and hope
God is able to use those moments we decide to disobey
Consequences provide strength for whatever's coming our way

A life without mistakes would be wonderful to achieve
But sin entered our lives long ago with Adam and Eve
Mistakes, even bad ones, come with a positive, though
God can take our biggest misstep and use it to help us grow

We are all people completely and seriously flawed
Sometimes stumbling along on our way closer to God
Working to get better every day is the recipe it takes
Knowing that growth is fueled by a lifetime of mistakes.

Harmony at 30,000 Feet

We've all been up there, above it all at 30,000 feet
The view so different when seen from this lofty seat
The hustle and bustle of earth just seems to disappear
As we peacefully float through the wispy atmosphere

This big ball we live on becomes a patchwork of shapes
Circles, squares, and rectangles adorn the landscape
A mosaic of colors adds to this hodgepodge puzzle
Some of the shades bold, some more subtle

Tiny little cars move along roads that stretch to the horizon
The flat plains and rolling hills give way to mountains risin'
Rivers wind like giant snakes across the thirsty land
A mile-long train adds to this panorama as only it can

Small villages appear and disappear as we cruise along
A ranch stretches for miles; the open space just seems to belong
In some sections, trees provide an ornate canopy
Soft, wispy clouds accumulate on the way, like cotton candy

Absent is the noise, the sound of auto, sirens, and factory
No guns popping off, no arguments, no fights in this potpourri
What we have instead is quiet and peace in this welcome reverie
It all seems to fit together, this moment in complete harmony

Wouldn't it be wonderful if we could live like this on earth?
If it could happen that way, what would it be worth?
Maybe when God planted us here, it's what He had in mind
That our living together would be harmonious, peaceful, and refined

So what do we have to do to make this happen and all get along?
With everything harmonizing together like a well-written song
May I suggest that the picture can be made complete
If we just imagine we're cruising at 30,000 feet.

Heeding the Call

In the movie, the Lion King, Simba, is the chosen one
He cannot run away from his destiny, who he's to become
Initially he takes the easy path, escaping to a foreign land
Only after much soul-searching, does he begin to understand

He knows he must return to take his rightful place
The challenge will be difficult, but one he must face
His father is there in the quiet to encourage him on
And applauds from afar the renewed character of his son

Simba returns to his homeland to do what he was called to do
It's a task he takes on not just for himself, but for others too
And when all is said and done, he follows his father's legacy
Taking up the mantle of leadership and claiming his destiny

Aren't we a little bit like Simba, wanting to run away
When things get more difficult than we can face each day?
When we just can't seem to clear failure from our mind
The mountain before us just seems too imposing to climb

But then there's the call from our Father, the heavenly one
And He reminds us of the sacrifice of His only son
He tells us all the strength we need will come from Him
Just be bold and obedient and He'll carry us to a win

And so we step into our destiny, never looking back
With God at our side, finding the courage we once lacked
And as we tackle our fears to claim the brass ring
We'll forever have a bond to the story of the Lion King.

Hierarchy of Faith

Many of us are familiar with Maslow's Hierarchy of Needs
Starting with physiological and continuing through love and esteem
A humanistic approach to be sure, topped off with self-actualization
But if you think it's all up to you, you're sadly mistaken

God has a different hierarchy---one of faith and belief
At the lowest level is atheism, only believe what you see
God is a fantasy, a crutch and we can live by only bread
And when we die, there's not a Heaven; we're just dead

The next level is those agnostics; they don't really care
It matters little to them whether or not God is there
They just go about their daily routine with no thought
As to whether the followers of Christ are right or not

Next up are the intelligentsia, the readers of all that is written
They are the academics; winning the debate is their religion
Their brains work overtime, but there's nothing in the heart
They just like to dazzle you with the knowledge they impart

We have the baby Christians who may have accepted Christ
But ingest no solid food; what's in the bottle will suffice
They just never arrive at the point of studying God's Word
They rely on others and hit-or-miss things they've heard

There are the ones who attend church on holidays---the CEO's
They may have some elements of belief, but it's mostly in repose
They just never seem to understand the relevance of the holiday
And when the service ends, they continue to go their own way

There are those who believe they can earn their salvation
How good is good enough is always the burning question
They often exhaust themselves doing good work for others in need
But they're driven by guilt, not the Holy Spirit's seed

Then there are those who've asked for forgiveness from Him
And asked Jesus to come into their heart and wash away their sin
Their life is forever changed; a new person in so many ways
And Death is not looked upon as the last of their days

The followers of Jesus learn to praise Him and pray in His name
Inside and outside, people can see they're not the same
Their priority is to become more like Christ in every way
Knowing He will stand in for them on Judgment Day

These are the true believers at the top of the hierarchy of faith
Love and forgiveness rule their hearts and not an ounce of hate
They realize death is a new beginning with the Lord, not an end
That they'll live forever in His house from the day they ascend

So climb Maslow's scheme if you believe all is under your control
Believing your own ambitions and success will make you whole
But, as for me, I'll do my best to become more like Christ
And reach the top of God's hierarchy, no matter the price.

Holding Hands with God

I remember when everything in life was new
And I couldn't be sure who or what to hold onto
Just a kid, there was much I didn't understand
But I always had the security of my father's hand

That hand was always there to guide through the crowd
Bringing calm to an atmosphere overwhelming and loud
There was safety as I reached for his hand to direct my feet
Avoid the rushing cars and escort me across the street

In childhood, that hand often pulled me back from danger
And protected me from the unknown of an approaching stranger
One of the scariest times was in the dead of night
That touch was so calming and always soothed my fright

Holding hands with my first love was a moment of bliss
Often followed in short measure with that first kiss
Holding hands at the altar is a time to remember
A feeling of oneness to cherish then and forever

But there's the hand of another to which none can compare
And it's been there steering my choices year after year
There were times I'd let go and move ahead on my own
But when trouble came, I'd look for God's hand to hold

I've strayed off the path many times, wandering lost and alone
I'm so thankful His hand was there, the one I've always known
The one that brings me back and takes away all anxiety
The one I want to hold on to through all eternity

My earthly father's hand was there, just the right touch
When I look back, I appreciated its comfort oh so much
But I can't meet life's challenges now and fulfill God's plan
Unless I walk with Him and work with Him, holding hands

His gentle hand has guided me through times good and bad
The times of great rejoicing and the times of the "Great Sad"
I don't need Him just when there are troubles to overcome
I'm holding hands with Him every hour until my days are done.

How God Speaks to Us

Most of us in one way or another have spoken to God
Even those who find the supernatural air waves a little odd
Even an atheist, in difficult times, will send up a prayer
Just in case they're wrong and there is a God up there

We love to talk and speaking to God is no exception
But a one-sided monologue is no way to make a connection
Our requests go up to Him, like we're on a one-way street
But listening is the only way to make this conversation complete

So just exactly how does God speak—in a big booming voice?
He certainly could do that, but that's not normally His choice
There are so many ways He can make us aware of His will
But first and foremost, recognize that He is God and be still

Let's remember this is the God of the Universe we're talking about
The One who created everything and knows us inside and out
He's not limited to the kind of communication we're accustomed to
He may speak to me in a way different from the way He speaks to you

One of the ways God speaks to us is through the power of creation
The planets in our solar system move in complete synchronization
Check out the rhythm of nature and you'll find complete harmony
It's the awesome power of God quietly speaking to you and me

Another way God speaks is the Bible, His personal instruction book
If you're reading it daily, there's no place else you need to look
Everything God wants to say to us is right there before our eyes
And we'll listen to what He has to say and apply it, if we're wise

He sent His Son to live among us when we were hopelessly lost
His love for us displayed through a horrible death on the cross
In a short 30 years, Jesus taught us everything we needed to know
His words are still relevant and speak to us from a time long ago

God could speak from the clouds if necessary to get our attention
But it would seem quite unusual to require that kind of intervention
He communicates very effectively, though, through prayers and thoughts
That solution we came up with, He placed in our brain, likely as not

Sometimes it's swinging doors that tune us in to what God discloses
One of those doors in life is opening while another closes
We may sense a nudge to choose one path over the other
And if we listen and respond, it's the right choice we'll discover

And let's not forget that God may be working through your friends
You may be following a course that can only lead to a tragic end
They may have prayed to God about your difficult situation
And were led to provide you with counsel and inspiration

In the Old Testament and New, there's the impact of visions and dreams
A pretty dramatic way for God to communicate His direction it seems
But God has so many ways to talk to us and make us understand
That He's in control and all we need to do is listen and follow His plan

God sometimes makes His will known through circumstances
He puts us in a position where there can be only one answer
It might not even be the answer we would have preferred
But we're compelled to move forward in obedience, undeterred

And what about our pastor's message each and every week?
Don't you think it's another way for our God to speak?
Isn't it amazing that his message, inspired from afar
Seems, at that exact moment, to hit us right where we are?

Music is another way as we lift our voices in praise
Each song will impact each of us in much different ways
If it brings a tear to your eyes and stirs your heart
You can be sure it's a message that God wants to impart

In the Bible, much is written about wonders and signs
But the ones He sends to me are a much less dramatic kind
It's the double rainbow at the end of a tumultuous storm
Or the majestic hawk doing a flyby in the early morn

You may feel called to take on a challenging new role
It's a calling that goes deep into your being, stirring your soul
You may resist for a while, but eventually you'll hear it
Because it's a direct line from God through the Holy Spirit

These are just some of the ways God chooses to communicate or talk
And we'd be wise to listen if we're going to walk the walk
You won't be able to recognize His voice through the worldly fuss
But if you'll just be quiet, you'll learn how He speaks to us.

I Remember You

You weren't trying to impress anyone, but I remember you
I took note of all the small things I saw you do
A woman frail, approaching the entrance to the store
You going out of your way to hold open the door

Picking up trash on the street that came from a passing car
Happy to contribute to any effort without being the star
Delivering a meal for someone whose luck was down and out
Showing love and compassion for those who live without

The driver in the parking lot, wanting in the traffic flow
You waving him ahead, though your time was expresso
The neighbor next door who needed a helping hand
And you responding like a trusted handyman

Being a listener when nothing else would do
Only a empathetic ear was needed, that you knew
In his later years, the way you treated your dad
Holding your kids tight to relieve the hurt or sad

How your marriage was the most important thing in life
There being nothing at all you wouldn't do for your wife
How you were always there to support a friend
Showing it was you on whom he could depend

This world is full of pessimism, anger, and despair
But you showed the need is strong for someone who cares
People are hurting and trying to figure out what to do
And it's no secret it's your kind who pull them through

Like Jesus Christ, you've set an example for me to emulate
And when the situation arises, I hope I won't hesitate
That if I'm in a quandary about what to say or do
I'll pause a moment, take stock, and remember you.

I Woke Up This Morning and I'm Not Dead

What shall I do with this day that lies before
What adventure awaits as I walk out the door
I hope I'm ready for whatever lies ahead
Because I woke up this morning and I'm not dead

Will I meet someone I've never met before
Or will it be an old friend from way back yore
I hope I'll learn something new, as it's been said
Because I woke up this morning and I'm not dead

Will it be some kind of calamity that's in store
Or some kind of victory causing my spirit to soar
Maybe I'll delve into a book that I've never read
Because I woke up this morning and I'm not dead

Will I be a blessing to someone who needs my help
Bringing satisfaction like I've never felt
I hope I don't just lay there, lounging in bed
Because I woke up this morning and I'm not dead

Will it be time with family---fun and so well spent
Will it start with a quiet prayer heaven sent
The opportunities are limitless, a to zed
Because I woke up this morning and I'm not dead

I know God is there and will direct my path
I pray that He showers me with love, not His wrath
If I but listen to His calling, I know I'll be led
Because I woke up this morning and I'm not dead

Maybe the day will be routine, nothing new coming my way
In any case, I still expect it to be a wonderful day
I plan to take it one day at a time, not look ahead
Because I woke up this morning and I'm not dead

Will the world be a better place when this day is done
Will I bring into someone's dreary life a little fun
I hope my focus is not on me, but others instead
Because I woke up this morning and I'm not dead

I'm waiting on you, Lord; what's your plan
My life today is completely in your hands
Father, give me this day, my daily bread
Because I woke up this morning and I'm not dead.

Iron Sharpens Iron

No man is an island says poet John Dunne
We cannot really live unless we have someone
Man does not live on bread alone
Others into life's tapestry must be sewn

Left to solitary, life brings but misery
We may be free, but there's no liberty
Reading may bless us with some learning
But sharing of ideas keeps our soul burning

We're a social animal, needing community
Anxious to engage others at every opportunity
A table for one is a lonely and depressing sight
A life without fellowship is dark as night

I think Solomon says it best in Proverbs 27
Iron sharpens iron is an important lesson
No one knows everything; only God does
And those knowing nothing, never was

We can all learn immeasurably from each other
Whether of the same or another color
We come together with different perspectives
And even long-held positions may be affected

We're better for having been sharpened in wit
Gaining wisdom from others bit by bit
Benefitting from what others have to say
And using that knowledge for the rest of our days

The Lord recognized early on that Adam needed Eve
And believers need others who also believe
The world would have us doubt our faith otherwise
But iron on iron strengthens us against all the lies

It's true, we can accomplish much on our own
But there are limits to achievements alone
God built group dynamics deep into our DNA
Knowing that iron sharpens iron; there's no other way.

In Full Bloom

The Dogwood tree– serene beauty in full bloom
God's caring, loving touch realized
In its presence, peaceful solitude looms
And anxiety, depression and anguish dies.

The Dogwood is not master of its own
Boldly and brashly proclaiming its flair
Rather preferring not to stand alone
But simply adding glorious strokes to what's already there.

Incredible isn't it that once only a seed
With love and nurturing and care
It poked through the earth, became the reed
And continued to develop and grow from there.

Next a sapling, at once vulnerable and frail
Needing staking and tethered support
To protect it from the whims of nature,
Wind, rain, hail –things of that sort.

Then, one Spring, there is the breakthrough
A single blossom is followed by several more
A small beginning, hardly worth the view
But a mere hint of the potential in store.

In Springs to follow, the sapling becomes the tree
Developing branches seek new paths to the sun
Flowers everywhere for the world to see
And gloriously, God's work is done.

Hopefully our children are like that Dogwood
And our love carries them through the growing pains
That we support them the way parents should
And help them cope with the winds of change.

Nurturing them as they grow from that tiny sapling
To the wonderful young men and women they can become
Branching out into new worlds and grappling
With all challenges; backing down from none.

Teach them, like the Dogwood, they don't need to be the star
Their presence alone adds immensely to any group
Tell them to be content just being who they are
Working with others to complete the loop.

Like the trees behind the Dogwood stand firm in support
Give them the belief they can reach for the moon
Trust them to their ambition and dreams; don't cut them short
And that glimmer of potential will reach full bloom.

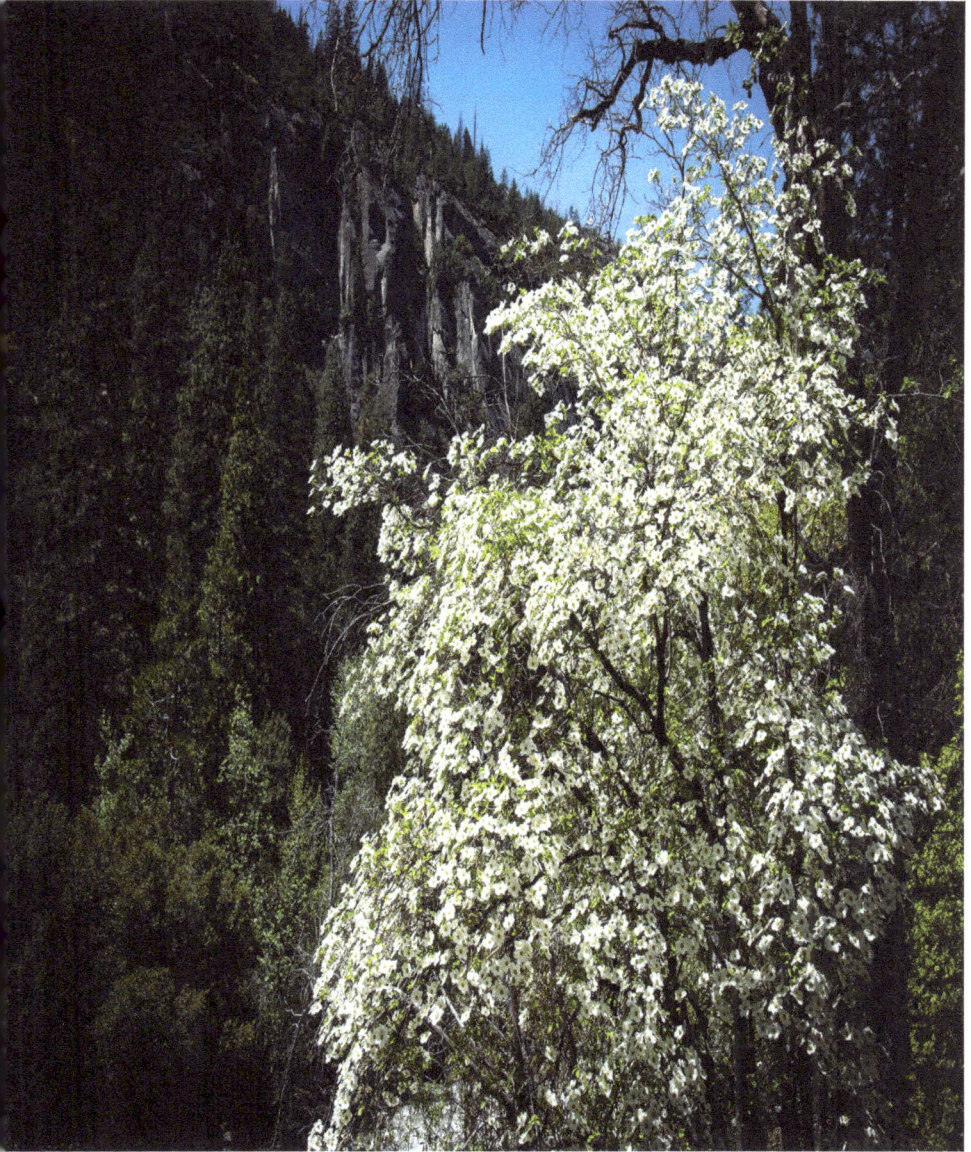

It's The Heart

Not the brain
Not the intellectual exercise of a genius IQ
Great minds often achieve worldly fame
But can't imagine how to be born anew

Not the eyes
What we see can be so deceiving
Satan in many forms, master of disguise
But faith in the unseen can bring true believing

Not the mouth
Treachery lies in every corner, said and unsaid
Words better smothered, find their way out
Dispensing not compassion, but distress instead

Not the ears
The truth is evident, but we don't listen
The Holy Spirit communicates, but we don't hear
Our internal receiver just seems to be missing

Not the circumcision
That under Jewish law was such a part
Rather an internal change was Paul's vision
A circumcision alright, but one of the heart

The heart is where it all begins
Is it a hardened and sealed off place
Or has it rejected Satan's call to sin
And freely accepted God's amazing grace?

When the Holy Spirit calls your name
And you're not sure just where to start
Invite Him in; accept the change
He will lead you if you just open your heart.

It's You God Wants to Send

A miracle is an event not explicable by natural or scientific law
Those recorded in the Bible leave us with a sense of awe
The feeding of the five thousand and the parting of the Red Sea
Turning water into wine at Cana and Lazarus to vitality

God certainly has the power to turn a miracle at any time
Creation and The Flood--- amazing events that come to mind
When all the best minds throw up their hands and call it spiritual
You can be sure that God is at work, bringing forth a miracle

We still acknowledge miracles today when there's no other explanation
And we've eliminated every other alternative from consideration
It's the terminal cancer patient who gets a clean bill of health
The patient in an extended coma who begins to speak for himself

There are other events we'd probably not put in the miracle category
They are amazing, but happen without the same measure of glory
It's the unexpected check that hits your mail at just the right time
Conversations with a close friend that shift your personal paradigm

It's the neighbor who brings you a hot meal when you're down and out
The gift that arrives when troubles are more than you can count
The chance encounter with a stranger who makes you laugh
Just when the world has taken your attitude to half staff

If you look at the times when a blessing came through, I think you'll discover
That it wasn't through your own efforts, but the efforts of another
It was God sending someone to lift you up and sooth your distress
Relieving your burden with understanding, empathy, and finesse

This is the way I believe God responds to most of our prayers
It's not generally a miracle performed that shows He cares
It's that quiet voice that whispers in someone's ear
That they are the one who can make some problem disappear

Sometimes when a friend needs help it's clear as a bell
At other times God's message doesn't come through nearly as well
But He'll keep reminding us until we finally listen
And take action on someone's desperate condition

I'm sure we can look at numerous times along the way
When a calling brought hope to us for another day
And just when we thought no one really cared
There was God sending someone in answer to our prayer

So be attentive and listen when that voice comes to you
Telling you who's hurting and suggesting what you can do
You won't be able to ignore it, whether stranger or friend
You're not a miracle worker, but it's you God wants to send.

Lean Toward the Light

Have you ever wondered why a barrel cactus leans to the south?
It's as if it's reaching for something it can't live without
Biologists will tell us it's the sun's life-sustaining rays
That the plant seeks and causes it to bend this way

It's no secret what plants need to flourish and grow
To rise up strong and dazzle us with their floral show
Fertilizer will be necessary regardless of terrain
And nothing survives without the blessing of rain

It got me to thinking-- what is it we need to spiritually grow?
What is it that nourishes our faith and feeds our soul?
What is it that makes us strong against the tempest wind
To resist Satan's urgings and the temptations of sin?

To the world Jesus was a beacon, a light on the hill
When we turn to the light, we turn to our Father's will
In throwing off our chains, we find all we'll ever need
And experience the peace and joy of God's only seed

Like the plants, we need nourishment feeding our roots
To move according to God's will and good works produce
The recipe for growth can only be found in God's Word
His instruction book shows us where and how we can serve

But growth in the Spirit cannot happen without Godly rain
It cascades over our bodies and washes away the pain
By ourselves, it's not something we can set in place
This rain is the lifeblood of forgiveness and we call it grace

So our growth has a lot in common with the plants you see
And we could probably further extrapolate this analogy
But suffice it to say that spiritually we'll be doing all right
If we just accept His grace and lean toward the light.

Light up the World

Did you ever notice life is full of contrasts?
Things are either moving slow or moving fast
The extremely wealthy and the extremely poor
Those content with less; those who want more

The patient one and the one who can never wait
Arrogant versus humble; love versus hate
The gentle one versus the one in your face
The one laid back; the one at a frenetic pace

The difference between the truth and a white lie
Young or old; the hearty laugh or heartfelt cry
Knowing what's wrong and knowing what's right
There is some gray, but it's mostly black or white

The most dramatic contrast of all is darkness and light
Light rules during the day and darkness the night
But light and darkness aren't just contrasts; they're adversaries
They have nothing in common, no similarities

Have you ever watched how a cockroach behaves?
In the dark, he's doing what he does, unafraid
But turn on the lights and he zooms to the nearest hole
Staying alive for another day is his only goal

Darkness associates itself with gloom and evil deeds
Light, though, has joy and happiness as its seeds
Darkness provides cover for all manner of despicable acts
And deals in fabrication and half-truths instead of facts

Darkness is the realm of Satan, the Evil One
Light is the realm of Jesus Christ, God's only Son
Jesus said I am the light of the earth
Follow me and you'll have life for all it's worth

Darkness can prevail as long as there's no light
But even the smallest flicker illuminates the night
Satan has no legitimacy, no rightful place
Standing next to the glorious glow of God's face

We all have a light to shine in the darkness as well
As ambassadors, God had given us quite a story to tell
There are dark corners everywhere for you to mine
So turn on that bright light of yours and let it shine

God will be with you, supplying all the power you need
Walking beside you to help you succeed
And to Him it will be like finding a precious pearl
You, doing your part to light up the world.

It's Written in the Stars

I have to admit I'm in love with a good analogy
Exposing concepts we previously could not see
Things that we may not completely understand
Can be brought to light with a simple sleight of hand

This biblical analogy finds its roots across the sky
So let's take a look and I think you'll see why
It all starts with God at the center, much like our sun
It's where everything originates, where it all comes from

God is for eternity and for our purposes, so is the sun
Both are an awesome source of power for each day run
Without either, the world we know comes to an end
And there's no chance it would ever start up again

Next we have the moon, reflecting the sun's light to charm us
Like the Son, Jesus, bringing light to impenetrable darkness
Sometimes the moon is just a sliver or disappears altogether
As does Christ when we turn away and ought to be better

There are the planets that revolve precisely around the sun
They all have names and we know each and every one
I think those are the disciples of yesterday and today
Every movement revolves around doing things God's way

There are the clouds that block our vision of the sun and Him
Those are the times we walk away, turn our backs, and sin
Occasionally, Satan disrupts our faith walk with an asteroid
But God steps in and the threat is diverted or destroyed

Last but not least, witness the cavalcade of stars in the sky
Even on the darkest night, they induce a natural high
I believe these are God's angels, twinkling with their song
And assuring us we are safe in His arms, that we belong

It's all displayed there for us, across this limitless expanse
And not even the smallest detail is ever left to chance
From the earth to the moon to Jupiter and Mars
What God wants us to know is written in the stars.

Like a Child

Innocent, trusting, excited over little things
A song in their heart they're willing to sing
Humble and awed by what they don't understand
Impossible challenge; they still think they can

They are wide-eyed and inquisitive right from the start
Bringing unquestioning faith and a joyful heart
They've not been cynicized by the world's concerns
Have an unequaled capacity to experience and learn

They respect authority, with only a few excursions
To mother and father, they are more joy than burden
They show us that laughter absolutely is the best medicine
And we never tire of watching their daily shenanigans

They run to father or mother when they skin their knees
And what parent can resist requests that begin with "please"?
They go through their days seemingly without worry or care
Knowing their parents, their protectors, will always be there

Time has no relevance to the things they like to do
And they respond immediately to praise and "I love you"
Their minds are unencumbered with worry and fret
They run free as a deer and setbacks quickly forget

We all know who it is that steals our heart, makes us smile
And pleases the Father with their innocence all the while
Jesus said, "You must become like a child to be with me"
Come with a heart that's pure and a spirit that's free

The Lord is also waiting for you with love and open arms
He's there to protect you from any disaster or harm
All you have to do is ask for forgiveness and freedom from sin
And He'll be there to welcome you, as you run to Him

We, the adults, are supposed to be the teachers of Christ
But children often teach us more of what it means to be nice
So if you're drifting from the Lord and things are a little wild
Step up your humility, simplify, and come to Him like a child.

Little Things

Little things, little things, little things
How often have you heard little things matter?
And yet we worry mostly about the big things
How much wealth, influence, and power can we gather?

How big is our house and how luxurious our car
Do we have 4K TV and Alexa as our techno toys?
Maybe we've forgotten what made us just who we are
By looking to the big things to provide our joy

European trips, Mediterranean cruises, and country club venue
If we could just savor the next big thing, we'd be in clover
Restaurants where we don't even understand the menu
As life moved on, the big things just seemed to take over

Interestingly though, I think it's pretty much a fact
That it's the little things our hearts fondly caress
They stick in our memory bank whenever we look back
And realize everything else was mostly meaningless

What do you think a person regrets more on his death bed?
That he should have spent more time at work with his boss?
Or the love and concern for his family, left mostly unsaid
Precious moments there was no time for, moments lost

Those moments were many, but seemed like so few
Frolicking with the children in the swimming pool
Camping trips, finding nature exciting and new
Those wild and crazy times when we all acted like fools

The first years of marriage, struggling as husband and wife
We were poor, but we never let that dampen our spirit
We were just too happy living out the simple life
If there was pain, love was there and wouldn't hear it

Common courtesies, heartfelt gifts, opened doors
Favorite songs, slow dancing, laughter never ending
Those things warm our hearts right to the core
Anniversary moments and for no occasion, flowers sending

When gourmet dining is having pizza with friends
When nothing can beat popcorn and a movie
When exercise is a hike in the woods, your soul to cleanse
And when just being together anywhere is groovy

But the biggest little thing of them all
Whether the mood is happy or blue
Whether child or adult, bound to enthrall
These three simple little words—I love you

There's nothing wrong with big things kept in perspective
But they're not the things of love that make our heart sing
In our later years, when we're just being reflective
Remembered with fondness will be the little things.

Living on the Mesa

We who live here in this Sonoran desert landscape
Have basically three choices in which to habitate
There's the valley floor where most choose to stay
Congregating mainly in cities to work and play

Some choose a much higher elevation, the mountain clime
Usually in smaller villages, a simpler life with less crime
The weather features cool summers and winters with snow
Relationships are tighter and go way beyond "hello"

In between, there's the mesa as a place to set up shop
It's basically a mountain with the summit lopped off
It has some advantages for living if the truth be told
Security, no flooding, and neither too hot or too cold

There's an analogy here which is interesting to explore
The ups and downs of living are the basis for this metaphor
Christians must demonstrate how to deal with both joy and sorrow
People are watching to see how we handle the highs and lows

I have to admit I'm an admirer of those who radiate peace
Those who turn everything over to God and all anxiety release
Their successes don't take them to the highest mountain peak
Nor do they succumb to the lowly valley when things look bleak

It's as if God has placed them on the mesa to live with Him
And their calm demeanor, without a word, just draws people in
They have that something that others want a piece of
They beam with faith and hope, but the Bible tells us it's love

Living life on the mesa is a perfect analogy for our walk with the Lord
Where we know we're safe, that we trust in Him and His Word
We can turn the tribulations of life over to Him, heart and soul
Knowing that living on the mesa lets Him be in control.

Look Up

"Look down, look down" sings prisoner, Jean Valjean
A sad refrain with all sense of dignity gone
And he continues "Don't look 'em in the eye"
In Les Miserables, it's his heart-wrenching cry

The Bible says, to the mountains I lift my eyes
From whence comes my help; my hopes rise
There's no help coming from below the ground
So why not look up instead of looking down?

But then we all seem to be lowering our gaze
And it begins at even the earliest of age
Discipline a child and watch as his head drops
Looking down is indicative of just being distraught

We carry this on, this lowering of our sights
And it doesn't matter if it's day or night
There are people we encounter on the streets
But with heads down, they're ones we'll never meet

As we age, the problem becomes even worse
It just seems to be the octogenarian's curse
We watch our steps carefully, not to fall down
And we look at our feet as we shuffle around

Technology has added fuel to this downward glance
We work the I-Pads and I-Phones as if in a trance
Even at dinner sometimes we just work those thumbs
Have we improved even a bit when all this surfing is done?

But on those rare occasions when our head's lifted
We can savor some of the sights our God gifted
Allow yourself to be mesmerized by golden sunsets
And snow-crested mountains are as good as it gets

Clouds of all kinds will paint the daytime art
And the nighttime stars will warm your heart
The moon's glow will add its own bit of charm
You'll feel an optimism that deflects all harm

When someone needs help, they always look to the sky
With hands raised, they'll not look down and here's why
The God of the universe is waiting there to lessen their burden
When they look up to Him in prayer, it's virtually certain

Remember your earthly father coming home from some place?
You had to look up to see the happiness on his face
And it brought you a joy it was impossible to hide
Look up; your Heavenly Father waits with arms open wide

So why go around with your attitude down and out?
Look up, child and discover what living is all about
Make a change in your life; hop out of that rut
Your whole world will be better if you just look up

I believe God communicates in many different ways
That there are no coincidences filling out our days
I'm sitting at the coffee shop, sipping from my cup
And above my head is an ad that starts with "look up"

So I'm going to make a real effort to raise my head
Not casting my eyes down, but looking up instead
It will be a demonstration of everything that I believe
And I know my God in heaven will be absolutely pleased.

Look for the Cirrus

Whether we care to admit it or not our moods change
And the changes often cannot be explained
One day were soaring high and going with the flow
And the next day we're about as low as we can go

Anytime you're in serious need of some inspiration
Just look around at the many wonders of God's creation
Rainbows, mountains, flowers, and babbling brook
They're all there to marvel at if you just take a look

One of the many visual blessings of our amazing God
Are the many kinds of clouds, there for us to be awed
As a kid and even now, they stimulate my imagination
Bringing forth a moment of complete captivation

One would look like a castle, another like a fort or a bear
Maybe it was a lion, a warrior, or a pirate ship up there
For each one, I might see the picture and you would not
You would see something else, a totally different thought

The clouds may put on their show in a multitude of ways
Their display as varied as there are stars or the year has days
And each may have something to do with our mood
Creating either a tendency to smile or sullenly brood

Nimbus clouds are the dark ones we associate with fear
They often come with lightning and the thunder we hear
But they also bring to the plants and animals blessed rain
And its power and might remind us that God still reigns

The stratus clouds are like a blanket, an impenetrable sheet
It's like a door closing, making the loss of view complete
Because these clouds are often very low in the sky
Our glass may seem half full and we don't know why

Cumulus clouds are white, fluffy, a little like cotton balls
Our interest in naming their shapes is what so enthralls
We are not limited in any way in our ability to imagine
And, in the process, whisked to a place we've never been

But my favorite of all are the cirrus which look like a feather
They stretch across the sky, whimsical but banded together
Their finger-like projections seem to softly touch each other
They're connected like family or lover to lover

The cirrus are the happy clouds that elevate our mood
They're the peace and contentment our souls have pursued
There to remind us of all the blessings God has bestowed
To lift us from our worries, to smile, and to lighten our load

So when life is so difficult that you just want to give up
I pray for cirrus clouds to lift your spirit; overflow your cup
Life is often full of trouble and we need something to cheer us
So just raise your eyes to the heavens and look for the cirrus.

Miracles or Blessings?

The Bible has numerous references to "wonders and signs"
What we'd probably call miracles in our time
And there are blessings, a somewhat less fortuitous event
But also very much appreciated and still heaven-sent

A miracle is an event not explicable by natural or scientific law
Those recorded in the Bible leave us with a sense of awe
The feeding of the five thousand and the parting of the Red Sea
Turning water into wine at Cana and Lazarus to vitality

God certainly has the power to turn a miracle at any time
Creation and The Flood--- amazing events that come to mind
When all the best minds throw up their hands and call it spiritual
You can be sure that God is at work, bringing forth a miracle

We still acknowledge miracles today when there's no other explanation
And we've eliminated every other alternative from consideration
It's the terminal cancer patient who gets a clean bill of health
The patient in an extended coma who begins to speak for himself

Blessings, on the other hand, are not quite in the same category
They are amazing, but happen without the same measure of glory
It's the unexpected check that hits your mail at just the right time
Conversations with a close friend that shift your personal paradigm

It's the neighbor who brings you a hot meal when you're down and out
The gift that arrives when troubles are more than you can count
The chance encounter with a stranger who makes you laugh
Just when the world has taken your attitude to half staff

Blessings are much more numerous and come in many forms
They could be material or just a way through a particular storm
You may not even recognize how the blessing plays itself out
Until the story has been written in a way that leaves no doubt

Blessings are not guaranteed outcomes for the way we serve
But rather a portion of God's grace we don't deserve
They're not distributed on the basis of works or what we've learned
We receive blessings based on God's will, not points earned

So it doesn't really matter if it's a miracle or a blessing
We just need to accept the gift that God is addressing
And thank the Lord with appreciation each and every day
For who He is and the amazing love He sends our way.

Monks on the Hill

We've all seen them in their hoods and flowing robes
Somewhere on a mountaintop, a solitary life they've chose
Chanting and praying in the holiest of atmospheres
From a religious standpoint, they seem to have no peers

They may be Christian, Buddhist, or Hindu in their belief
Their holiness seems to be unquestioned and spiritually complete
They've left all the temptations and distractions of the world behind
Their walled-in monastery is a sanctum for a clean heart and mind

They seem to be the Godly definition of piety and peace
All worldly possessions and concerns have been released
Each day is immersed in tranquility, calmness and spiritual
Their worship so reverent you almost expect a miracle

But is that what Christ had in mind in his declaration
Aren't we are to go and make disciples of all nations?
The monastery walls may be overflowing with contrition,
But what about the responsibility to the Great Commission?

But before we dismiss the monks as secure in their bubble
Are we that much different there inside our holy huddle?
We don't have impenetrable walls built of mortar and block
But our spiritual walls are just as solid, are they not?

Like the monks, we're more comfortable with our Christian friends
It's unnerving to meander outside the safety of our spiritual den
Often the reaction of non-believers is in your face and scary
And we retreat to the security of our spiritual monastery?

Christ encouraged us to be out front and bold in our faith
That's extremely challenging in this world of vitriol and hate
But if God is for us who can stand up against His will
Stand firm and don't become one of the monks on the hill.

My Prayer For You

This is my prayer for you
That you find love in all you do
Comfort on those difficult days
Hugs when things don't go your way

That you have friends to brighten your being
And beauty in everything you're seeing
Confidence when you're in doubt
And rainbows when the rain gives out

Smiles when sadness intrudes
And laughter to change your attitude
Courage to know who you are
And faith to follow the brightest star

Patience when you're in a hurry
Belief that overcomes the worry
Golden sunsets to warm your heart
And turning to God at each day's start.

No Room at the Inn

The Baby Jesus, at birth, had to be laid in a manger
They didn't know who he was; just another stranger
It was not a warm and cozy bed that he slept in
Why---because there was no room for Him at the inn

History has not treated the innkeeper very well
For shunning the Messiah, was he destined for Hell?
Couldn't he have found some kind of accommodation
For God come to Earth offering hope and salvation?

But aren't we a lot like the innkeeper? No room for God at our inn?
All rooms reserved and occupied much to our chagrin
So that when the Lord knocks on our heart's door
We turn Him away like the innkeeper we abhor

So who or what has filled up all the rooms of our heart?
And can't we clean them out and make a fresh start?
Busyness has lived there for a long, long time
And Greed has positioned himself at the head of the line

Pride has taken up the top floor, the penthouse suite
Living up there with his buddies, Boast and Conceit
Deception has taken up residence just down the hall
Gossip and Slander, permanent residents and that's not all

Selfishness and Control are also welcome guests
Envy, Vanity, and Judgment occupy the rest
So we're really not so much different are we now
From the innkeeper we criticize and disavow?

But if we can purge from our heart these lingering sins
We'll have plenty of room for our Lord to come in
And He won't have to be knocking again and again
We'll have booked a lifetime reservation just for Him.

Oh, Holy Spirit

Oh, Holy Spirit, how can I find faith
Surrounded by a world of angst and hate?
Please come and rescue my wretched soul
My life is lost and spinning out of control

I want to do the right thing and yet I do not
I turn away from all the things you've taught
I judge people when I know I have no right
And the world's values corrupt both day and night

I lust after beauty, even if it's only a look
And I confess I forget what's in your instruction book
I've violated most of the Ten Commandments
Either as an outright sin or at least, intent

I wear various masks; I don't want people to see
What a failure I am and the extent of my hypocrisy
I proclaim to be a follower of Christ and yet I sin
My shortcomings are many; I don't know where to begin

So, Holy Spirit please be with me in a fresh new start
I come before you with a penitent and open heart
This is my prayer and I know you will hear it
I'm waiting here for you this day, oh, Holy Spirit.

Pandora's Box

It's a legend of Greek mythology that people know even today
And they would tell you the story is irrelevant in so many ways
You know the one where Pandora opens the box or jar
And all the evils of the world are released near and far

Death, destruction, perversion, murder, and rape
Lies, gossip, envy, and greed, they and more all escaped
Closing the box left only one thing to help us cope
Way down at the bottom was the blessing of hope

When we look at our world today these evils are all there
They seem to be growing in strength, pervasive everywhere
The nightly news is full of tragedy, hopelessness, and fall
Where can we run to; can we get away from it all?

Where does the answer lie; can we change and learn?
Can these evils somehow be put back in the urn?
Or are we relegated to committing the same old sins
Is hope still in that box and can it be revived again?

There is a place where we can find the hope we need
It's not in a box or jar, but it is hope's only seed
It's the Bible and its message is even more pertinent today
The One who died for us is ready to listen if we just pray

Politicians don't have the answers; the government is broken
Follow the words in red and how clearly they're spoken
Our Lord is coming to restore His kingdom, He told us so
And that promise is the only hope we need to know

Yes, Pandora is just a fable, but the hope can still resonate
The evils of this world can be put back; it's not too late
Jesus told us "I am the life, the truth, and the way"
Only He can bring the hope that we crave today.

Pennies in the Parking Lot

Many times you've probably walked across a parking lot
And noticed a penny on the ground, likely as not
Did you take a moment to bend down and retrieve it?
Or did you just think it's not worth the effort and leave it

In my case, I know I've often just left it on the ground
In too big a hurry to even think about bending down
After all, it won't buy anything; it's mostly worthless
An annoyance that should be taken out of service

But if you look a little closer, the penny has a lot to say
On it, a great President, Lincoln, is prominently displayed
On the left side, you'll see the crux of our founding, "liberty"
And above Lincoln, "In God We Trust" for all to see

On the back side you'll see "United States of America"
It's like a reminder of unity past, a different era
"E Pluribus Unum" reminds us of how we were once together
One unified voice that made us stronger; made us better

So you see, that worthless penny contains quite a bit of history
And why we treat it with such disrespect is something of a mystery
It represents many of the values we Americans hold dear
A reminder of a time when our principles were crystal clear

The population of the United States is about 323 million souls
All accounted for by headcount in the latest census polls
What if each of us picked up one penny a year in the parking lot
And dumped all those pennies into one big charity pot

By my calculation, that would be 3.2 million dollars---plenty
To justify each of us stopping on our way to pick up that penny
Think of all the good that could be done for those in need
And at no cost to us, such a simple kindness in deed

Sometimes I wonder if God himself throws those pennies there
Just to test our sense of humility and the brotherhood we share
Maybe our life has become too haughty or maybe we just forgot
The intrinsic value of the pennies in the parking lot.

Presents and Presence

Presents, who doesn't like to receive presents?
Or feel the love and thoughtfulness they represent?
They're tangible evidence someone really cares
An expression of devotion to the friendship you share

And Christmas is the perfect time to give and receive
One of the threads of a relationship never to leave
It's a magical exchange that brings joy to life
Whether it's a child, neighbor, friend, or wife

But in all this excitement of the Holiday Season
We must never forget the underlying reason
Of why we celebrate this wonderful time of year
Why our spirit rejoices with feelings of good cheer

You see you can't celebrate Christmas without Christ
His gift came with the ultimate love and sacrifice
The "mas" in Christmas translates to "more"
So the word itself has "more Christ" at its core

So I trust that your Holiday will be filled to the brim
But take a few moments to remember and honor Him
Enjoy what is one of the years' most momentous events
And fill it with presents, but also with His presence.

Priceless

Famous artists, even non-aficionados know their names
Da Vinci, Monet, Picasso, and Rembrandt
Their works considered masterpieces of lasting time and fame
Their brush strokes attract our eyes and our hearts enchant

Their works have been counterfeited, stolen, and idolized
Purchased by collectors and galleries for enormous sums
The texture and depth they bring to the canvas surprise
What could possibly compare with what they've done?

May I suggest a different kind of canvas and work of art?
The Lord produces it every day on the medium we call sky
Visually pleasing, it moves the soul and touches the heart
With an incredible capacity to astound and beautify

There's the magnificent rainbow signifying the end of the rain
It's an awesome spectrum of colors brushed across the blue
And when it dissipates, we can hardly wait for it to come again
And grace us once more with its breathtaking rendezvous

There are the billions of stars painted across the blackish night
No human endeavor can match the depth of this cosmic excursion
There's a peace about this starscape that makes all seem right
And we lose ourselves, like a child; it's a complete immersion

There are the sunrises and sunsets, each better than the last
The clouds are painted with colors beyond our wildest desire
The sun burning off the morning mist is unsurpassed
The fading sun sets the mountains and canyons on fire

The moon, all by itself, could give the canvas its due
Whether it be perched on a ridge in its silvery sheen
Or casting the earth in an uncomfortable and eerie hue
And adding mystery and uncertainty to a shadowy scene

Add to the painting the brilliance of Venus or a shooting star
Maybe the Big Dipper, Orion, or the Milky Way
And you can lose yourself; even forget where you are
Because it's the greatest work of art; a complete dossier

What's described here is only the incomparable earthly piece
What God has promised no eye has seen or no mind conceived
In Heaven, His glory will be a visual and spiritual feast
In this promise, lies the beauty of tomorrow for those who believe

So what value would you place on God's brush strokes?
If available at an auction, you'd pay handsomely, I'd guess
If a da Vinci is worth millions, let's be honest here, folks
What God paints cannot be bought; it's absolutely priceless.

Real Happiness

Life, liberty, and the pursuit of happiness
Endowed by our Creator for nothing less
But where do we find this happiness we're to pursue?
And is it the same destination for me and you?

Is this happiness found in any material things?
And is it strictly the purview of queens and kings?
How about a mansion with acres of land?
Surely, that could bring happiness, if anything can

What about reaching the top of the corporate ladder?
Enemies were made, but does that really matter?
Maybe it's that college degree; that framed paper
Or the professional honors that came much later

How about that shiny sports car you bought with cash?
Or with the scratches and dents, did your joy fade fast?
Could it be dining at the most posh restaurant in town?
Or did the bill that followed quickly bring you down?

I think we can all agree material things come and go
But the things of lasting happiness I think we know
That lifelong partner who stood by us through the years
Celebrating our victories and calming our fears

Those memories, still residing in the corner of our minds
Joyful and precious moments we'll never leave behind
What about when you finally discovered real living
Finding it not in receiving, but rather in cheerfully giving

What about those friends who stuck by us even when we failed?
Guiding us through the rough spots; helping us prevail?
They just weren't smart enough to leave us by the way
But stood by us till we found the joy of a better day

Real happiness requires equal measures of peace, hope, and love
The kind that can only be provided by our Father above
When we finally understand that His love can forgive any sin
We'll find that peace and happiness that can only come from Him

The joy that God can bring is here on earth, but also eternal in scope
And knowing that we will be with Him forever brings joyful hope
So when the Founding Fathers talked about pursuing happiness
Maybe it's both the earthly and eternal kind they were trying to suggest

We all know that life is not a bed of roses or ice cream and apple pie
There will be days when our best-laid plans simply go awry
But if we tune into His grace during both the good and bad times
It will be a life of liberty and real happiness that we'll find.

Resurrecting America

One of Webster's definitions of resurrection is a resurgence or revival
We all know about "The Resurrection" that portends eternal survival
And there's been nothing since to remotely compare to that event
But several times in our history, we've come together as if heaven sent

Our fore fathers structured our country on Christian principles
But we've drifted away to such an extent they're barely visible
We disdain prayer and have taken God out of public places
We've lost concern for each other and it's written on our faces

We fight and bicker, even resort to calling each other names
There's class warfare even though our life goals are largely the same
Instead of "us" in our dialogue, there's likely a lot more "me"
And as years go by, there seems to be more ways we disagree

But every once in a while The Lord uses circumstances to call us back
When the problem can't be fixed with psychology, consultation or Prozac
And people finally admit the trouble is beyond what they can handle
When they've considered all other alternatives, explored every other angle

Situations that come to mind are world wars and the Great Depression
Times when everyone had to sacrifice and everything was in question
The 9-11 attack is a more recent example of catastrophe at our door
In each of these times we came together as Americans like never before

E. Pluribus Unum was more than just a slogan, many became one
We were united in our attitudes and worked together till victory was won
With perfect strangers, we extended our help to show we cared
And even the doubters could be heard talking to the Lord in prayer

In short, it was a resurrection to when this country was a band of brothers
When we put aside our personal ambitions in order to help others
And when we do this it is proven we are a force to be reckoned with
That the American response to a crisis is more than just a myth

Our latest challenge is the coronavirus and we will overcome it as well
Just how that story will play out and how we change no one can tell
But neighbors are helping neighbors and families are reconnecting
Governments and corporations are part of the American spirit resurrecting

Heroes are everywhere, serving in our hospitals and in their homes
Reaching out to others who cannot get out and are suffering alone
States better off are sending their ventilators to other states
And everywhere we look, concern for others has replaced hate

So when this crisis is over and things return to normal once more
Will we have learned anything about how to treat those next door?
Will we have made necessary changes to keep ourselves protected?
Will we return to the Lord in prayer and truly become resurrected?

Or will we revert back to the ugliness evident in recent years?
I pray we give it all to the Lord to trust in Him and calm our fears
That we acknowledge again our fore fathers so long ago had it right
That everything starts with God, His love, His power, and His might.

Seeds of Doubt

Are you a Christian whose faith is pretty small?
You believe there is a God, but that's about all
You come to God mostly in troubled times
But forget about Him when everything's fine

Your prayers are short, requisitions are rehearsed
You don't expect answers and prepare for the worst
You may really wonder if there is a heaven or hell
And there just seems to be so many doubts to dispel

If we're honest, we all have some measure of doubt
And our culture uses every trick to get us to sell out
But God is bigger than anything they can produce
And He is waiting for you to turn His power loose

The smallest seed in biblical times was the mustard seed
Yet it could grow, with nourishment, into a small tree
Big enough that birds could come and perch on a branch
Build a nest there and make a home if given a chance

So even faith that's less resistant to sin's temptation
Can, with time, grow strong enough to handle every situation
And provide sanctuary for those who would come to Christ
The Holy Spirit's power bringing their faith to new heights

Jesus said in his teaching "Nothing is impossible with God"
Bring your petitions to Him and prepare to be awed
Without Him, even the smartest man can do nothing at all
But even the weakest faith can grow and answer His call

So regardless of where you are today in your faith walk
You too can become as solid as Peter, the Rock
From that small seed great branches can sprout
And remove any and all traces of the seeds of doubt.

Shed the Shackles

I'm sure you're familiar with Plato's Allegory of the Cave
Three prisoners shackled to the wall of this dark enclave
Since birth, they've only seen shadows on the opposite wall
Those shadows represent in entirety their knowledge of all

Then one day one of the prisoners finds a way to break free
He leaves the cave to a truth he could not previously see
At first, he is blinded by the sun and it's painful to his eyes
Nothing visible through the pain no matter how hard he tries

He longs to return to the cave where familiarity reigns
A reality he knows, there's comfort in the chains
But he is somehow drawn to the sun and its clarifying appeal
Ever so gradually, his eyes adjust and new truths are revealed

But once the darkness of the cave has been overcome by the sun
A whole new life of understanding and wisdom has begun
But when the prisoner returns to the cave to tell his friends
They just cannot accept the news or even try to comprehend

They do not understand venturing out of the cave to finally be free
Preferring to spend their lives in chains through all eternity
They even begin plotting how to eliminate the one shining the light
Because they only believe what's on the wall and directly in their sight

Isn't this allegory a lot like Christ come to earth to save the lost
Bringing light to a world of darkness and at a terrible cost
His radiance so bright they could not see He was the Truth and the Way
And many are still in the cave of shadows and lost to this day

It's a leap of faith that leads us out of the darkness and into the light
Only the awesome power of the Lord can illuminate the night
So if you're still chained to that wall of darkness, there's hope for thee
Shade your eyes, step into the light, the truth will set you free

Christ came to earth and took on human form, to show us what's true
There's a life outside that dismal cave that's both exciting and new
You'll wonder why it took you so long to end this aberrant behavior
Shed the shackles and heed the calling of your Lord and Savior.

Shimmer By the Light of the Lord

I love to sit on our patio, gazing at our fountain
It's on a par with looking at our magnificent mountains
There's something about the sight and sound of running water
That seems to take away the stress any day has authored

I can appreciate the fountain's serenity any time of day
But sunset brings out its beauty like a New York ballet
I can sit there and be enveloped by its mesmerizing sound
Water bubbling up and, just as quickly, cascading down

Sunset is an amazing addition to this spectacle, though
As light hits the fountain the water shimmers, adds to the show
The shimmer and glimmer draws attention for all to see
The mind drifts to a time when life was easier and carefree

You can see the same shimmer on an afternoon lake
It's an effect that only water, light, and God can make
So it is as well with the meandering river or babbling brook
And to feel its peace all you have to do pause and look

I wonder if I shimmer when God shines His light on me
And when people look I wonder what person they see
Do I present a picture of peace and attract them to Christ
Or do I lose the glitter of His love and amazing sacrifice

God can turn any ordinary person to one displaying His glory
You can be a reflection of Him by simply telling your story
No matter that you're not perfect and still a sinner
People will pay attention---in His light, you shimmer

Some may not even notice you and just pass on by
But if you're shimmering, they'll stop, not understanding why
They'll know there's a reason it's you they're drawn toward
And one day they'll know you shimmer by the light of the Lord.

Ship of Faith

What if God asked you to do something considered borderline insane?
Would you do it even if it seemed the loss might far outweigh the gain?
What if you weren't skilled and didn't understand the work to be done
And you had some doubts about the outcome or the victory to be won?

Has God ever asked you to do something that seemed beyond your reach?
Maybe something you didn't think you could learn, let alone teach
Did you react by standing firm, using the age-old question, "why me?"
Or did you get busy with the task at hand for an outcome you could not see?

Think about Noah, building this monstrous ark high on a hill, no water near
An awesome task even for a young man, but Noah was up in years
Even if he had some shipbuilding experience, it was nothing on this scale
But he set to the task, knowing that God would not allow him to fail

It's hard to imagine he did not suffer rejection, persecution, and ridicule
But when it was all done and the Lord had his way, who was the fool?
It took years for Noah to obey, put up with the insults, and complete the task
I'm guessing he had his doubts right to the end about what God had asked

But the door was open for Noah and his family and he chose to walk through
Do you do the same when the door is flung wide open for you?
It must have been sweet vindication for Noah and joy he could not restrain
When the clouds formed, the thunder struck, and it began to rain

So how do we respond when the task is great to which we've been called?
Do we say, the task is too hard, the water's too deep or the mountain's too tall
Or do we plunge right in obediently, praying that the Lord will show us the way
And that He will provide the lamp at our feet on even the darkest day?

What Noah built was more than a floating zoo; it was a monumental ship of faith
The ship's size alone was a testament to the perseverance it would take
Noah had built his trust on God's promise that his family would be saved
That they would survive the battering of the waves and the watery grave

How's your ship of faith doing? Have you secured everything to the main beam?
That would be Jesus Christ, holding it all together in even stormy extremes
Will your ship even stay upright and stable when the ocean pounds its side?
When the persecution comes, will the Lord be your strength and your guide?

Will you stand firm when the world attacks you and mocks your beliefs?
Or will your ship end up on the rocks and be destroyed on the reefs?
God gave detailed instruction to Noah on how to build a great ark
Likewise, the Bible shows us how to follow Jesus and leave our mark

All we have to do is heed His instructions, trust and obey
And our ship will be on solid ground when the waters go away
Like Noah, whose ship came to rest on Ararat in answer to prayer
Our Lord will bring us safely home and we'll anchor there.

Simmer in Prayer

Solar tea is made with water and tea caressed by the sun
Its essence is released as a gentle, unhurried process is run
You cannot brew a proper tea with a satisfying taste
Using extremely hot water and tea made in haste

Likewise my Master is at work and I'm simmering as His tea
He has many different ways to bring out the essence of me
It's a slow process as He teaches me the wonders of Him
Removing the bitter taste that comes with the intrusion of sin

Sometimes I try to take over the process, brew my own me
The result of this free will is expected and easy to foresee
This brew, when finished, is rancid; not at all drinkable
And going my own way completely unthinkable

I am steeped in His love and slowly I'm beginning to see
That He has just the right process for the flavor of me
And all I have to do to make me a brew beyond compare
Is go to the Lord in worship and simmer in prayer.

Skip Another Stone

Have you ever stood by a river, flat stone in hand
And tried to skip it across all the water to dry land?
It takes not only a good throw, but a perfect stone
To skip that rock multiple times until it reaches home

Did you ever notice that you fail more times than succeed?
Most times the rock just falls to the bottom among the weeds
But then, when least expected, a rock skips safely to the other side
And you celebrate with a joy you just cannot hide

You can't throw the stone like a pitcher in baseball
You have to release it sidearm and that's not all
It involves bending at the waist and a flip of the wrist
Athleticism, yes, but not the skill of a perfectionist

Isn't this a great metaphor for the challenges we face?
We're going to fail more times than we win the race
But once in awhile, our "stone" hydroplanes across the river
And with God, we bask in the glory of "stand and deliver"

And we don't have to be perfect in the way things are done
With less than perfect form, the race can still be won
Find a great idea and with enthusiasm, pitch it across
Even if it falls to the bottom, all is not lost

Look around and find a better idea, a better stone
One that will skip and skip until it reaches home
You'll never know if it will reach the opposite shore
Unless you pick up another and give it a go once more

Some of the most successful people failed multiple times
But they knew the value of persistence of body and mind
And knew that eventually they'd bring it all home
By not being afraid to just skip another stone.

Something More

There's more to living than just surviving
More to success than just arriving
More to spirituality than just believing
And more to happiness than just achieving

There's more to satisfaction than just status and cash
More ways to profit than greed unabashed
More to music than just the dance
And more to a marriage than just romance

There's more to sport than the winning goal
More to relationships than who's in control
More to courtesy than opening a door
And more to growth than just wanting more

There's more to golf than just breaking par
More ways to demonstrate just who you are
More to helping the poor and those in need
Than just the checkbook to help them succeed

There's more to education than just a degree
More to faith than what you can see
More to believing than the mind and the intellectual
And more to God's Word than just conceptual

There's more to prayer than elegant words
It's what's on your heart that God prefers
There's more to talking with God than endless requests
Applauding His mercy and grace pleases Him best

Jesus said his reason for coming to earth
Was to have life and to have it for all it was worth
He returned to the Father to show us the way
Until we join Him, we're to live to the fullest each day

There are deeper levels to reach in just about every situation
And I think it all started with the beginning--creation
Just as the universe presents endless new adventures to explore
So in life, there's always that element of something more.

Spiritual Glasses

The Bible tells us to put on the full armor of God to metaphorically speak
The breastplate of righteousness and the shield of faith for the weak
The sword of the Spirit, the belt of truth, and the helmet of salvation
Once suited up for the warfare to come, praying in all situations

But if we're to resist Satan in all his forms, in all his disguises
We need to add something else to defeat the one God despises
It's not Excalibur, the white horse, or arrows for the coming clashes
You may be surprised that it's not a weapon, but a form of glasses

Glasses, you say, are you feeling all right or are you out of your mind?
But these are no ordinary glasses; they're quite a different kind
They're not reading glasses or those that protect your eyes from the sun
They're not bifocals or transition lenses with stylish frames overdone

These glasses have a focus that's not on the things of today
They won't let the distractions or troubles of earth get in the way
These are spiritual glasses that will put you on bended knee
And they're focused not on this life, but the life to come---eternity

They're the same glasses David wore when he faced the Philistine giant
It was not on his power but on the Lord's that he was totally reliant
So it was with Daniel, trusting in the Lord to close the lion's jaws
And rendering it impossible for the lion to strike with his powerful claws

Then there's Shadrach, Meshach, and Abednego in the furnace of fire
Saved from a nasty death even though the flames roared higher
And don't you think Moses wore the glasses when God parted the sea
And then collapsed it on the Egyptians, drowning their invincibility

Did you not see the glasses Jesus wore while hanging from the cross?
Surely, they allowed him to see the victory over death, not the loss
To see that his time at the right hand of the Father was near
That his ascension was at hand; a vision made perfectly clear

When we put on these glasses, we see things not of this earth
But the New Jerusalem, eternity, and what God's promises are worth
We can look beyond all our fears, challenges, and all other things
Focus on the cross, God's will, and the power he brings

So if you're being tossed around like the waves on the sea
Maybe your relationship with the Lord isn't what it's supposed to be
If your life is in turmoil and you find it difficult to rise from the ashes
Maybe it's time to focus on Him and put on those spiritual glasses.

Still You Loved Me

Life on the dairy farm was not easy and I complained
That I was not blessed to be with the others, mainstream
I'm sure you heard my cries of woe and misery
But my attitude and whining aside, still you loved me

My teen years were not easy; we didn't have a lot
And the girls I wanted turned away, likely as not
You could have punished me or at least left me alone
But still you loved me and always welcomed me home

The college years were a lost cause with its liberal bent
I didn't care about your Son or why he was sent
I was climbing Maslow's hierarchy; it was all about me
But through all the deceit and rejection, still you loved me

In my career, it was material possessions, the money god
Even though I knew this pursuit was limited and flawed
I justified my existence by the toys I could accumulate
But still you loved me and were willing to patiently wait

During all this time you were not my number one
You took away from my pleasure and interrupted my fun
Attending church was work when I just wanted to sleep in
But still you loved me; it was my soul you were seekin'

The years have passed and I've finally turned to Christ
I recognize what he did for me and at such a horrible price
And as I look back now, it's no longer a mystery
I'm so thankful that through it all, still you loved me

You sent the Holy Spirit to keep me on track
There's no reason at all for me to ever look back
My place with you is prepared, secure in eternity
For it's through your amazing grace that still you loved me.

Sunday is Coming

There are many religions which all stand by what they believe
They may even claim all other religions are being deceived
But Christians hold one thing that's different from all the rest
That Christ arose from the grave, achieving victory over death

Satan probably crowed when Jesus suffered and died on the cross
But God in heaven had too great a plan for all to be lost
And while what happened on Friday was ugly and stunning
Final victory would be His because Sunday was coming

Our world today can also be ugly and in much the same way
Lies, fraud, and cheating are still part of each day
It can be depressing and hard to follow Jesus, the King
When crime and deception infiltrate everything

We're not beaten and crucified like Jesus, not even close
Our suffering is more emotional, fearing rejection the most
But when we feel like giving up, and finally succumbing
Our strength comes from knowing that Sunday is coming

The Biblical principles Jesus taught us while here on earth
Are being questioned at every turn, as to their worth
We're doing our best, Lord, to carry the torch, keep on becoming
Knowing that Friday will pass and Sunday is coming

We believe we will follow Jesus one day and live again
Because He made a path for us to join Him despite our sin
That even with all the corruption, distortion, and cunning
We can be optimistic and resilient because Sunday is coming

So when someone puts you down, keep your eyes on the prize
Because one day, as Jesus promised, you too will rise
To your Master's outstretched arms you'll soon be running
Because all your Fridays will be over and Sunday is coming.

That Changed Everything

To some you were just a baby conceived like many before
To the Pharisees, you weren't the one they were looking for
You didn't fit the mold of the warrior, the all-conquering King
But when you arose from the dead that changed everything.

To some you were just a carpenter, plying his trade
Handiwork creations perhaps proudly displayed
May have thought these were the only skills you'd bring
But when you arose from the dead that changed everything

To some you were just another prophet of zealous fame
One of those with a following, but no lasting name
Most couldn't imagine you could be the real thing
But when you arose from the dead that changed everything

To some you were just a preacher with tricks up your sleeve
Nothing more than a magician some would believe
At times even your apostles would not your praises sing
But when you arose from the dead that changed everything

But now we know you came to earth us sinners to save
Death would not have its way in that earthly grave
And now we know you were truly the Messiah, the King
Because when you arose from the dead that changed everything.

That Day

Lord, this is a troubled world we live in
And some days, it takes all we have not to give in
But when we're about to concede to the world's way
You take our memory back to That Day

That Day you struggled up to Golgotha hill
Lugging that cross according to your Father's will
Beaten unmercifully with whips tearing at your flesh
A time when your apostles just weren't at their best

They didn't know you, that's what they said
Too afraid that they too might wind up dead
Watched in horror as you were nailed to the cross
Not understanding your mission of saving the lost

The punishment you endured for our salvation
Providing a way for us out of eternal damnation
Thorns on your head and nails through your hands and feet
Blood that flowed to make God's redemption complete

You were faithful to the Father and we were awed
Suffering the agony of a human, even though you were God
You could have stepped down from that cross at any moment
But that was not to be part of the lamb's atonement

By comparison, our troubles exact such a small price
We just stand in disbelief at your loving sacrifice
Our worldly tribulations all fade to a place far away
If we just think about what transpired on That Day.

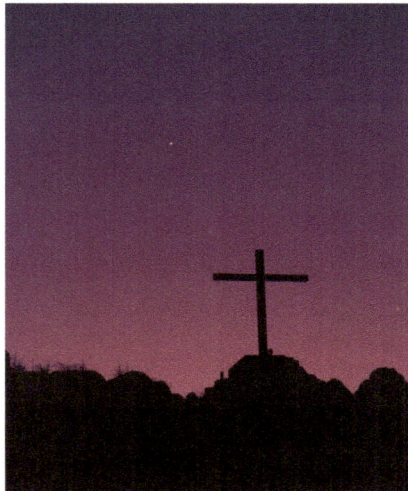

That Ordinary You

The night was ordinary in every way
The dark overcame the light in the usual way
Maybe there was a gust of wind somewhere
Or maybe there was a hint of chill in the air

Maybe it was a beautiful night in December
But it wasn't one likely you'd remember
Not one of surprise to keep you awake
No fiery red sunset over a peaceful lake

The sheep were on the hillside bedded down
Most eyes closed, not making a sound
Just lumps in the night, silhouettes
Loved as a master would love his pets

The shepherds were there, destitute and poor
None of their clothes bought at a department store
They were a simple and nameless lot
Knowledgeable and worldly they were not

Ordinary night, ordinary shepherds, ordinary sheep
Nothing you'd write in your journal to keep
Were it not for the Lord, this night would pass
Without anything to remember or anything to last

But the Lord deals everyday with the ordinary
And his hand quickly transforms it to extraordinary
The common becomes uncommon for a reason
And 2000 years later we celebrate the season

Suddenly, the sky explodes; shepherds on their feet
Sheep, once content, are a chorus of bleat
The night would be ordinary no more
His Son had come to earth as prophesied before

That's God's workplace—simple, ordinary, and weak
The ones who need him most are the ones He seeks
All of our limitations, our imperfections, and sins
That's where the power of the Lord begins

So, if you'll just bring Him your ordinary stuff
His awesome strength and love are more than enough
To transform your life, make it exciting and new
And you won't recognize that ordinary you.

That's How I know You're My Lifelong Friend

You've been there through it all, thick and thin
Sharing in my laughter and forgiving my sins
Lifting me from depression and raising my joys
In the midst of turmoil, quieting the noise

Holding me accountable when I've run off the track
And in every difficult situation, having my back
You loved me when I couldn't be loved
And you prayed for me to the Father above

You lifted me up when I just wanted to be blue
In all situations, you helped me do what I needed to do
You helped me sort out the truth amidst all the lies
Your counsel was always helpful, timely and wise

It hasn't all been easy street that I can attest
But your effort to help me was always your best
During the most troubling times, on you I depend
And that's how I know you're my lifelong friend.

The Last Crossroad

We come to an intersection and stop at the light
For a brief moment, our life crosses another's way
The light changes and we both move on
Never a thought given to this encounter of the day

In our lifetime, we have thousands of encounters
Most are like this one, nothing to even remember
They don't fill the tapestry of life, not the smallest thread
Not a fire started or even a smoldering ember

But there are other crossroads that raise the heartbeat
What's important in life, bringing meaning to it
Material trappings and money take a back seat
There's something intangible and you want to pursue it

The Bible talks about the most notable crossroad of all
When man and woman are united and become one flesh
Each becoming incapable of functioning on their own
Together they make each day exciting and fresh

It may seem that this crossroad is purely random
That it was happenstance, but that is far from the case
It was providence that brought about this meeting
And it was blessed from the beginning by God's grace

The Lord put them together according to His plan
And it seemed like neither would ever be alone
But God's ways are sometimes hard to understand
And one day He calls one of them home

It is a sad day, but also one to foster hope
Coming is the greatest crossroad of all time
When you meet again in the company of the Son
A glorious crossroad with lives forever intertwined

The tapestry forged together in life is now complete
The Lord's hand apparent in what we now understand
Magnificent in its wholeness, but each thread discreet
We're at the last crossroad of God's elegant plan.

The Answer's in Your Backyard

Are you someone who just can't accept the idea of creation?
That there has to be some kind of humanistic explanation
That somehow all the right stuff randomly came together
And complex DNA strands were formed without a director

Look around at the interconnected structure of nature today
Could a random series of events have really set it up that way?
Isn't it more plausible that it's the result of some intelligent design?
That all the pieces were carefully crafted by some superior mind

The answer to this age-old question might be in your own yard
Take a look around at the wonders; you won't have to go far
A perfect time to contemplate all of this is at the onset of Spring
When God does His absolute best to showcase everything

Isn't it amazing that everything a plant requires is in one seed?
That in that one tiny element is all the information it will ever need
To sprout, to grow, and to become whatever it was meant to be
And to beautify our world in ways astounding to believe

Take a stroll around your backyard and note the wonders you see
Buds develop and flowers open in this springtime jubilee
The colors encompass every hue and shade of the rainbow
And what causes their delicate petals to unfold no one knows

The types of flowers are as varied as the imagination can conceive
Roses, lantana, lilac, lupine—just a few of thousands you'll see
Even the prickly desert cactus puts on its own kind of show
With great big beautiful blossoms they're able to bestow

Notice how the bees gather at the flowers to fulfill their mandate
And in satisfying their desire for nectar, help the plants pollinate
Hummingbirds, in their probing for nectar, do exactly the same
God put these intricacies together so it would glorify His name

Nature is an intricate web of plants, animals, insects, and birds
The way it all fits together makes the idea of happenstance absurd
Everything seems coordinated in accord with some master plan
And how anyone could think this was random is hard to understand

So question if all this was created by God if you must
But if you just look around, your mindset will have to adjust
You won't have to study biology or even walk that far
Sit on your patio and observe; the answer's in your backyard.

The Big Room

As I stood there in this enormous room, feeling terrified and small
I looked around and couldn't be sure it was a room at all
The walls were more like barricades of light and went on forever
My heart was pounding and I hadn't felt like this, ever

Then I looked up, saw this big board and gasped at the display
There for all to see were my sins from birth until today
They were scrolling across the screen in an endless show
The ones from just yesterday and ones so long ago

The sins of my life were all there in excruciating detail
The times I swore, lied, and cheated so as not to fail
The times I gossiped about others, including friends
The people I offended and never made amends

The people who were different that I ignored without a thought
The times I celebrated stealing something and not getting caught
The times I drank too much and justified going wild
The times, as a grownup, I acted like a child

The times I grumbled because things weren't going my way
Forgetting to thank God for each and every day
Turning away instead of helping those in need
Worshipping the money god with unabashed greed

Coveting the material possessions of my neighbor next door
His big house, fancy car, bank account and more
Not stopping to realize I had also been immensely blessed
No matter, the grass was always greener I guess

The times I refused to let humility be my guide
Bragging about accomplishments with unmitigated pride
Believing that somehow it was all under my control
And that I didn't need God to make me whole

The list went on and on and on until I could look no more
How was it someone knew everything about me right to the core?
I thought I had lived a good life, a good person all right
So why was I ready to run; ready to take flight?

My face turned red, my palms began to sweat, my eyes to tear
All of my friends were watching with me, worsening my fear
I began to choke, the breaths coming short and strained
Where was I and why was it so out of this world and strange?

Then I saw Him in the distance, dressed in white and all aglow
What was the penalty He had for me? I deserved it I know
I remember reading that death is the wage of sin
I could not speak; no place to hide, no place to begin

As I was about to say I'm sorry for everything I'd done
He opened His arms and said "Welcome home, son"
Tears welled up in my eyes and I fell to my knees
I knew it was too late, but I said, "Lord, forgive me please."

Then I noticed what looked like blood flowing down the screen
And as it did, it was erasing all my transgressions we had just seen
I stared in disbelief at what I did not understand
Then it dawned on me—the blood of the Son Of Man!

And then they were there, thousands of angels, that is
They encircled us closely and I knew they were His
The songs of joy they were singing were like nothing I'd heard
The lyrics, though, came straight from the Word

I was dumbfounded as I looked one last time at the board
And all I could get out was "Thank you, Lord"
For the screen was blank, the sins were lost
Except for these words "Debt paid on the cross"

Then I was awake, was it a vision or just a dream?
The message was so vivid, though, I know what it means
It's a reminder that I am found where once I was lost
And that He gave it all up for me there on the cross.

The Lesson of the Long Spoons

I had a dream last night, one I'll never forget
An angel was guiding me on this learning trek
We went down, down, down to the lowest floor
Into this massive dining room through an open door

As I looked around there were all the trappings of Hell
What was surprising, though, was the tantalizing smell
Coming from this huge pot of stew and tickling the senses
Rendering any thought of abstinence completely defenseless

Then I noticed that the people were wasting away
Looking like they hadn't eaten for hundreds of days
They were wailing in their misery for something to eat
Craving for even a small portion of potatoes and meat

While I was trying my best to understand this dichotomy
The rest of the scene made the problem as clear as could be
Each were using long-handled spoons to get the food out
Spoons so long they couldn't get the food in their mouth

All across the room you could hear them moan and cry
All the more miserable because they weren't allowed to die
As we turned away, I was relieved to leave this picture of gloom
Up, up, and away we went to another similar room

The smell was the same, but the sounds were so much different
It was the sound of happiness-- laughter and singing exuberant
They had the same pot of stew and the same long spoons to eat
But their bodies were as healthy as any world-class athlete

The angel told me I was looking at heaven's table
That, with God's guidance, they were more than able
You see they had learned to thrive with their brother
By simply setting selfishness aside and feeding each other

When I awoke I had the lesson I'd learned clearly in mind
Not only for our brothers' physical needs, but also another kind
We must be careful to tend to their spiritual needs as well
To keep them from the clutches of the Evil One in Hell

Jesus said, "I am the bread of life, the Father sent me"
Whoever believes in me will never die, but live eternally
But you must share the Good News with your brother
The life you have found in the Lord, you must help him discover.

The Perfect Plan

Did you ever wonder what life might have been?
What would it be like if you could somehow start again?
What if your situation was totally different at birth?
Would you contribute more or less to planet earth?

I was born into poverty, but what if I was rich?
Would I be altruistic or just worship the money itch?
I was a country boy, but what if I was a city slicker?
Would I have climbed the corporate ladder quicker?

What if I was smarter, not just an average Joe?
What if I was educated at Harvard, not Buffalo?
What if I could have danced like Fred Astaire?
What if I had the means of a multi-millionaire?

But, on the other hand, what if I was born in another land?
Inhospitable places like Syria, Iraq, or Iran?
Places where a dictator's authority reigns supreme
Where the liberties I enjoy are just a dream

What if I had no home, just living on the street?
Every day a challenge for food and shoes on my feet
Sickness and exposure to cold a constant threat
Begging on the roadways for whatever I could get

Yes, the life I've lived could have been so much different
The things accomplished so much more or less significant
But when I look back, there's one thing I understand
There are no coincidences; it was God who dealt this hand

I'm right where God wanted me, what He ordained
And without Him, I know my life would not be the same
So instead of being wistful about what might have been
I'm just so thankful that, for me, God had the perfect plan.

The Olive Tree

There are so many amazing creations of our God
Just stand still, look around, and be awed
The mountains that rise up out of the plain
The cactus which can live with virtually no rain

The stars and planets all moving in synchronization
In a pattern that's remained the same since creation
How the animals have adapted in order to stay alive
The bees who are the key to how most plants survive

Then there's us, the most intricate earthly being stands alone
A living complex of veins, arteries, nerves, muscle, and bone
All systems controlled by the master computer, the brain
And how it all works together no one can really explain

We could pick out any organism now living on earth
And extol its virtues; what it does to present its worth
The candidates would be plenty, but you may not believe
If I ask you to consider the case of the olive tree

The olive tree has stood the test of time, longevity
2000 year old versions stand in the Garden of Gethsemane
There when Christ was betrayed by a treacherous heart
And it was an olive branch the dove brought back to the ark

The symbolism of the olive tree can be a guide in our faith
So many messages to show us how to live for Christ's sake
Among other things, it's the international sign of peace
A signal to lay down arms, start talking and all conflict cease

The steadfastness and perseverance of the olive tree is hard to refute
After years of drought, heat, and storms, it's still producing fruit
While its trunk and its bark may be gnarled and twisted
It is to be applauded for all the various attacks it's resisted

Admirable characteristics even for us--- challenged, but still resolute
We may be old and gnarly, but that shouldn't stop us from producing fruit
And to everyone around us, couldn't we just bring an aroma of peace?
Offering in our attitude an olive branch, all animosity released

The olive tree is able to survive by sending its roots deep
Grabbing nutrients and water other trees cannot reach
We too, as Christians, can survive in much the same way
Developing roots that go deep and connect to our Lord every day

The fruit of the olive tree produces oil when it's pressed
Oil that's treasured for food and health benefits it may possess
Likewise, Jesus was crushed and his blood poured out on the cross
And that blood is treasured as the way to the Father for the lost

So you see the olive tree provides us with quite a metaphor
For how we're to live out our lives; what we're here for
And regardless of our age, we can still accomplish good
Producing the good fruit that God always thought we could.

The Puzzle

Have you ever worked on a jigsaw puzzle to pass the time?
You know the 500-piece or 1000-piece kind?
Where it's the picture on the box you're trying to recreate
And it involves equal parts of motivate and exasperate

You usually start with piercing together the border
By doing this, you bring some structure to this disorder
From then on, it's finding pieces of the same color scheme
That you try to hook together to match the box scene

But how successful would you be if you had no picture?
Wouldn't you be frustrated with such a chaotic mixture?
And after minutes turned to hours with precious little success
Wouldn't you want someone to help you out with this mess?

Isn't that a lot like life as we try to put the pieces together?
Positioning one piece at a time to make the whole look better
And we don't know what the final picture will look like
We can only hope for a life that reaches the highest heights

But don't you know there's someone with every piece in hand?
Only He knows which pieces to hand you for His perfect plan
And we don't have to know how it all matches; how it ends
We just have to take the first step, place a piece, and begin

It's been said you don't have to have the whole staircase in mind
To, in faith, take that first step and begin your climb
So pick up that first piece and place it on the table
Listen to God; you may not have a clue, but He is able

We must be careful to not force a piece where it doesn't belong
Recognizing that our inclination to go it alone is all wrong
Because any piece that's misplaced affects the final whole
Even if it feels good for a short time to be in control

But if you follow His will, taking it one day, one piece at a time
There's no obstacle you can't overcome or mountain you can't climb
Gradually, the picture you're constructing will come into view
And you'll experience the wonderful life God created for you

The puzzle that's life is all put together in God's flawless plan
He holds the finished picture on the box; it's in His hand
There will be times when the piece He's giving doesn't seem to fit
But maybe all you had to do was trust in Him and just turn it a bit

When you step back and know you've completed the scene
God's power will reveal blessings like you've never seen
You'll look back on a life with all the pieces in place
And you'll understand the impact of His amazing grace

The blessings God provided will all come into view
And you'll realize the life He directed was only for you
He took all the pieces lying there in a confused muddle
And created a masterpiece that was your lifelong puzzle.

The Spirit Train

There's something nostalgic and relaxing about a train ride
Maybe it's the sense of history or the rolling panorama it provides
Maybe it's the clickety clack of wheels on rail that excites
Or maybe just remembrance of a simpler time that delights

The journey begins at some hub and moves station to station
And at each one, there's an option to jump off at that location
There's a peaceful feeling to the trip, maybe that's the appeal
A window on the world as we roll down the ribbon of steel

Maybe it's a connection to our spiritual journey that attracts
A vision that God is our engineer as we move down the tracks
This journey on His Spirit Train meticulously set in place
Offering undeserved love, choices, and amazing grace

Each station on His spiritual journey requires us to choose
At each stop there will be opportunity to accept or refuse
And if we make the complete trip, what a welcome it will be
Stepping off the train and onto the ramp of eternity

The first stop seems to be in the middle of the desert, nowhere
It's hard to believe that anyone is even found waiting there
But these are the lost souls looking for an oasis of hope
They haven't been able to find answers and their spirit is broke

Next we have the station of seeking the truth, "Discovery"
Maybe a time of searching or the beginning of spiritual recovery
It might mean opening God's Word for the very first time
And finding in His words something to cling to, a lifeline

The route proceeds to the next stop-- the station, "Admission"
It's where we admit our sinful life, one in critical condition
With it comes a prayer asking for forgiveness for all we've done
Admitting that on our own, we're lost and need the Son

The next station is the most critical sojourn---the station, "Belief"
We're on bended knee, asking for the Lord to provide relief
We acknowledge that Jesus is who he said he is, God's son
That we need his grace, mercy and relationship, one-on-one

The Spirit Train rolls on and we move to "Commitment", station 4
This is where we commit our life to Jesus Christ forevermore
Our stay here is not short-term; time to become more like Christ
It's a period of sanctification, learning about love and sacrifice

Once we've made all the stops, the Spirit Train heads for home
We embrace eternity and it comforts like the greeting "shalom"
They'll all be there---the apostles and the angels as we roll in
Singing hallelujah and applauding as we are welcomed by Him

Our sins have all been whitewashed by the blood of our Savior
We'll never have to pay for our erratic and disobedient behavior
We'll live in that mansion He promised us so long ago
Heaven is a mystery, but it will be amazing, this much we know

There is one problem on this glorious ride that lingers still
God made us aware of all that's in store, but He gave us free will
There's a long black train streaming the opposite way
It is an enticing, luxurious ride with promises that easily sway

The train is sleek and it's alluring to consider crossing the tracks
But once you board, the engineer, Satan, won't let you look back
To the riches and peaceful eternity of heaven you can bid farewell
This is an express train with one final stop, the gates of Hell

The Spirit Train requires work, commitment, and dedication
But the long black train is the easy path to eternal damnation
Choose the ride that will bring challenge, but save you from pain
You'll be eternally grateful you chose the Spirit Train.

The Stupid Years

Thank you, Lord for getting me through the "Stupid Years"
When You could not compete with the influence of my peers
Those years when I was absolutely certain I knew it all
I had a conscience, but it was mostly muted, as I recall

Mom would give me instructions not to do this or that
Whatever was taboo was the thing I couldn't wait to get at
I made fun of other kids who were different from me
The harm that I brought on them I just could not see

I drove recklessly, not even considering the speed limit
After all, I'd be late for some party if I didn't put a kick in it
When the girl said "no" all I heard was some version of "yes"
"No" was not part of my early vocabulary, I guess

I went to church, but I was just playing a bit part
The message hit the brain, but missed the heart
The mask I wore covered almost all of my ineptitude
Back then, I believed that somehow I fooled even You

When my life should have been busy chasing after Thee
Instead I was chasing advancement up the money tree
Trying desperately to keep up with the other boys
Accumulating a bigger bank account and adult toys

There were times, Lord, when I took your name in vain
I know my actions probably made you groan in pain
I didn't know the Ten Commandments were in your hand
And the death and resurrection I didn't care to understand

What's amazing to me is how You let me go on this way
Knowing that you could turn me around some day
That one day I would come to my senses and realize
That each life has meaning when seen through your eyes

You would not let me be a victim of my own stupidity
Instead you fostered a life of purpose and humility
I've heard it said "you can't fix stupid", but it's untrue
All we ever have to do is just turn it all over to You

I am so thankful, Lord, that you stuck with me through it all
That in later years I heard your voice and answered your call
That I can now look to you for forgiveness, not dread
And know for certain the truth of every word you ever said

I believe, Lord, that many youth are much like me today
Thank you for working with them to change their ways
Even though they think they're in control and just don't hear
I ask that you protect them, Lord, through the "Stupid Years".

The Wrong Wall

The ladder is there before us
And from early childhood we begin the climb
Better student, better athlete, recognition a must
Pulling ourselves up one rung at a time

There's college, certainly one of prestige
We need that plaque on the wall when the job's done
Our pursuit of excellence never does cease
And we pull ourselves up another rung

Our career begins and we play the game so well
Promotions follow; victories are won
Bigger house, fancier car, anyone can tell
We've pulled ourselves up several more rungs

Climbing ever higher, we swell with pride
Conversation centers around successful me
We arrange our trophies, side by side
The money god just won't set us free

Then, one day as we enter the autumn of our days
We wonder quietly, what has our life really meant
Why the emptiness, what's the legacy we've saved
And for our children, what message was sent

Then, without warning it hits like a bolt heaven sent
Hard to understand why we didn't see it at all
We're not satisfied with the rapid ascent
Because the ladder's on the wrong wall

Rather than the wall of self, try the service wall
What can you do to help your brother climb a rung
Be still, listen to that voice, and heed the call
And you'll find meaning in what you've done

You've heard it said, "better to give than receive"
And it's the little things that matter
There's no doubt these things you can truly believe
Just make sure you choose the right wall for your ladder.

Things I've Learned in Retirement

We've been in retirement now for thirteen years
They've been filled with a lot of joy and just a few tears
It was a happy day when we bid our career au revoir
The notes I've kept say this is what we've learned so far

The blue skies of Arizona are easy to get used to
There's no longer any pretense; you can just be you
No one's that important in retirement and the corollary
No one cares if you were a general, a surgeon, or a missionary

If you didn't know what your wife did all day or even how
You'll find out in retirement; they'll become your chores now
We are blessed beyond belief to live in this place
It's just another part of God's amazing grace

It's a lie that your golf game gets better the more you play
But your drives definitely get shorter with each passing day
Buying your own golf balls is a bummer, I've found
But finding a Pro V1 can be the highlight of your round

I miss work sometimes, but not enough to prepare my resume
Sunday nights are better because there's never a Monday
That briefcase and computer are no longer part of my being
And no definite schedule can be immensely freeing

Maybe in retirement I could really amount to something
But probably not, because I've perfected doing nothing
If you wait to retire until you have enough money and no fear
You're probably going to have a very long career

The best tasting wines may not be those of the prestigious label
Besides, we'll sample any vintage you put on the table
A glass of wine is better than an apple for keeping the doctor away
And there's a bonus---you can have more than one a day

No day is complete without a peanut butter sandwich
And happiness is not defined by the terms poor or rich
The beauty of nature is everywhere, day and night
Stop, take a breath, there awaits an awesome sight

We've gotten to know the parts of the body pretty well
Most of them have been replaced and we love to tell
To share every detail about the surgery and the doctor's name
And which pills you should be taking to relieve the pain

Everything is under the control of God
And nobody loves you as much as your dog
True friends are few in number, but they make life worthwhile
And you'll feel so much better with just a laugh and a smile

The crisis of today will be gone tomorrow
Friends elevate your joy and reduce your sorrow
There are still skills to be learned and books to be read
Just because we're old doesn't mean we're dead

Humility is difficult and pride hard to suppress
Whatever your wife's question, the answer is "yes"
Adventures are more exciting when shared together
And whatever you're really good at, someone is better

A man watching three games at a time may amaze your wife
She may not understand football, but she understands life
You can analyze things in your mind frame by frame
But your heart is better counsel than what's in the brain

Read the Bible and use it as your daily guide
You'll be surprised at what you find inside
Tears are a way of God cleansing your soul
And without Him in your life, you'll never be whole

Life is short, but eternity is a long, long time
Getting through life on your own can be an uphill climb
There are bad people, but there is many a good one
And we'd all be hopeless if God didn't send His Son

The retirement years are a great time for taking stock
Of just what's important and what is not
Of focusing on those things that really matter
And realizing that the rest of it is all just chatter.

This is My Prayer

I'm a sinner, Lord, but I want to be free
I'm prideful, help me live in humility
Illuminate my darkness with your redeeming light
Give me the wisdom to separate wrong from right

Bring love front and center, Lord, instead of hate
Bring forth the kindness that should not wait
Give me some of the patience of Job
Help me spread the seed you want sowed

Help me be truthful, dispensing with the lie
Make me unafraid of the day I die
To turn away from the love of money and greed
Not coveting the things that I don't need

Help me be a witness to the circle of influence I'm in
First and foremost, let them see me as a friend
Help me be joyful in all times, good and bad
Encouraging others when times are sad

Strengthen me, Lord, in my weakness
I'm nothing without your forgiveness
Help me find, Lord, my fruitful place
And shower me with your amazing grace

Help me, Lord, be the Christian you want me to be
So that those around me know I follow thee
Give me the words Lord that I need in prayer
I know you're listening in the great somewhere

Protect my family, Lord, keeping them safe and secure
And bring them closer to you with hearts that are pure
These are my entreaties to you, Lord and King
I know for certain you can handle everything

Make me, Lord, the kind of man who can be
With you and the angels through all eternity
I have no accomplishments on which I can stand
I'm totally reliant on your merciful hand

This is my prayer, Lord, on this day
That you would direct my steps toward your way
That you would help me be the man you created me to be
That I would be welcomed at the gates of eternity.

Three Sheets to the Wind

I am a sinner and like many, I'd prefer to keep my sins hidden
But I wanted to know for sure my failings would be forgiven
So I decided to list them all on three sheets of paper
And present them all at the same time to my Lord and maker

The first sheet, if there is such a thing, might be called minor sins
Not minor in God's eyes, especially since they happen again and again
There in my youth, but still unchecked and continuing today
The page was full and wanted more, this disobedience resume

On this page were both sins of commission and omission
When help was clearly needed somewhere, it was missin'
People begging for some kind of assistance were left in the lurch
It can be inconvenient to stop when you're on your way to church

The second sheet listed those sins of the more serious kind
Their impact on others didn't diminish with the passage of time
Several were held close to the vest and only God and I knew
The mistakes I had made that I could never really undo

This sheet was filled out by severity, not by the numbers
Things done in haste while my conscience slumbered
No thought at all as to whom or how it might affect
Driven by thoughtlessness and no measure of respect

Then there was the third sheet which was absolutely blank
And for that I had the future and father time to thank
There was the expectation that more sin was in the wings
Because ever since the Garden, it's what our nature brings

Holding these three sheets I asked for what I didn't deserve
That God would forgive me and my place would be reserved
The tears that flowed were proof I was open and contrite
And completely at His mercy to make our relationship right

At that moment, a gust of wind swept the three sheets away
And in that instant, the aroma was sweeter than any bouquet
I knew only through the Son could God absolve my sin
But my prayer was answered in full by three sheets to the wind.

Today is a Gift

Today is a gift
A blessing for sure
Will it be one to treasure
Or just another to endure?

Each day is an opportunity
The Lord has sent your way
Will you use it wisely
Or just let it slip away?

Time is racing forward
This day will soon be done
Will you fill the fleeting minute
With a full sixty seconds run?

Will you be receptive
To what God has in store?
Or will you go your own way
Like so many times before?

Will you appreciate the beauty
Of flowers, mountain, and brook?
Or will you be so engrossed
You fail to even look?

Will you encourage a friend
Not wasting another minute?
Or will you forget how they enrich your life
And how glad you are they're in it?

Will you be a blessing
To someone less fortunate than you?
Or will you just walk away
Convinced there's nothing you can do?

Will you look to the heavens
And contemplate God's awesome power
Be grateful that He walks with you
Each second, each minute, each hour?

Will today be the day
When you say "Yes, Lord, Yes"
I'm following You
With a heart full of thankfulness?

What if somehow you knew
That today was your last day?
Would you have a list of regrets
About what you failed to do or say?

Don't let this day pass
The sand is trickling through
Today is a gift
From our Lord to you.

Twelve Ordinary Men

They were just twelve ordinary men
Living out their lives in the simplest way
You wouldn't have chosen any of them
Blue collar workers we'd call them today

Several fishermen, a fanatic, and a tax man
What could we really expect them to do?
Either despised or of no account back then
What they were capable of no one knew

They had the greatest teacher in the world
But they couldn't grasp the essence of his mission
They listened but it was as if they never heard
These were not men of great speech or vision

They had intensive training for three years
And yet, at the crucial moment, they were lost
Denying they even knew him, they gave in to their fears
And watched in horror as their leader died on the cross

But God had yet to unleash his extraordinary power
They had no idea of what was coming; what was in store
The Holy Spirit would be sent at the appointed hour
And their ordinary lives would be ordinary no more

Like a tiny flame quickly becomes a raging fire when given air
These twelve took the Gospel to the ends of the earth
Their Great Commission was no longer one of despair
It was as if they had experienced a second birth

Aren't we like the twelve---just ordinary folk after all
Struggling to make a living; trying to survive
But not really living until we receive the call
And take up a higher reason to be alive

God has a purpose for each of us; a reason, a goal
The power of the Holy Spirit will show us the way
Follow the calling as the twelve did so long ago
And ordinary can still become extraordinary today.

Two Paths in the Wood

Two paths in the wood, running side by side
Exploring the world for just a short little while
Worn smooth by footsteps of laughter and love
Days that were joyful, if lacking in grace and style

The paths had character, trod deep and wide
Not a thought they would fade with the passage of time
But Father Time has his own plan for each life
The winds of change shift each to a new paradigm

The things we did along those paths, insanity
Youth has its own definition of how life should be
Nothing would I trade, though, for the trail we've run
The adventures we shared, you and me

The years pass and the paths begin to fade
Leaves and new growth begin to fill the way
But below it all, the memories refuse to perish
And as I uncover, it's those I'll cherish each day

Then one day the other path I could no longer find
I believe it's now in a new dimension up there
The day is coming when we'll re-open those paths
All the hurts will be gone and we'll run without a care

Your life has no small part to play in my memory bank
Whenever I feel bad, I think of our time together
And that moment of sadness is overcome by joy
And I'm thankful for how you made my life better.

We are Not

He is Eternal, He is Father
He is The Good Shepherd, He is Glory
He is Creator of everything we've got
He is Love and all of these we are not

He is All Powerful, He is All Knowing
He is Perfect, He is the Provider
He is the Savior, we've been bought
He is Righteous and all of these we are not

He is Sovereign, He is The Alpha and Omega
He is Grace, He is the Great I Am
He is Infinite, we're just a dot
He is Holy and all of these we are not

He is Justice, He is Mercy
He is the Healer, He is The Way
He is Lord, lest we forgot
He is King and all of these we are not

God said, "Be still and know that I am God"
We are to worship Him and be awed
He owns us and He owns our soul
So why do we even think we're in control?

Weaving Lives

The other night, in my dreams, I saw the Weaver
His looms were humming for every believer
The tapestries were masterpieces to behold
Intricately interwoven threads of silver and gold

I knew in an instant these were lives He was spinning
Some tapestries were nearly finished, some just beginning
The Master sat at the controls in this heavenly ballet
And smiled with each new soul that came His way

I looked a little closer and saw the tapestry for me
But it pleased me not in the least for what I could see
Yes, like the others, there was the finely crafted part
But there was also something there that broke my heart

The silver and gold were strung together in elegance
Flawlessly they moved together like some mysterious dance
But every now and then in the pattern was a major flaw
All of this beauty was brought down by the ugliness I saw

I stood there trying to understand what went wrong
Why didn't this section of threads seem to belong?
Then it hit me why these flaws so damaged the whole
These were the times in my life when I insisted on control

There were many times when I wouldn't listen to His voice
Mistakenly thinking what I had in mind was a better choice
He gave me free will and I too often exercise that blessing
The results, though, which benefit no one, are distressing

Suddenly I was awake and thinking about the dream
Its meaning wasn't subtle; it was like a laser beam
Trust in Him every minute, every hour, every day
Listen to that Voice, take it to heart, and obey

If I do all that, my life tapestry will be beautiful for all to see
And they'll know just who put it all together for me
Those flaws will give way to silver and gold if I'm wise
And allow the Lord to do what He does best, weaving lives.

What I Wanted

What I wanted was a childhood of riches; others envious of me
What I got was learning the value of all things through poverty

What I wanted was the affections of the most beautiful girl in school
What I got was someone to teach me the meaning of the golden rule

What I wanted was a flashy Corvette or a new Nissan Z-car
What I got was a Volkswagen bug without a roll bar

What I wanted, in order to impress all my friends, was a trophy wife
What I got was a wonderful woman who'd put up with me for life

What I wanted were sons who would play as hard as the rules allowed
What I got were daughters meeting every challenge and making me proud

What I wanted was the biggest and most luxurious house on the street
What I got was a debt-free house where friends comfortably meet

What I wanted was to be a basketball star or golfing icon
What I got was something so much more valuable to rely on

What I wanted was six-pack abs, Arnold Schwarzenegger physique
What I got was a very healthy body, if somewhat slow and weak

What I wanted was to be able to dance, really rock the floor
What I got was a slow waltz and not a whole lot more

What I wanted was to be the best in the world at anything at all
What I got was failure and picking myself up after every fall

What I wanted was a bank account that would match my pride
What I got was God teaching me that He will always provide

What I wanted was to ignore God, do my own thing, go my own way
What I got was God bringing me back to Him at the end of the day

The years have gone by and it is only now I realize
That most of my wants and cravings never did materialize
But all of my needs were provided by the Master's hand
And it's only in my senior years that I finally understand

For all the unsatisfied wants there was a lesson to be learned
And each was painful I must admit, as it took its turn
But I've grown so much, protected there under His wings
That I'm truly thankful He didn't give me any of these things

Only once was what I wanted and needed exactly the same
And it could only happen through the power of Jesus' name
For when He died on the cross and said, "It is done"
He provided eternity for me with the Father and Son.

What Would Love Do?

Words straight from the Bible, provoking thought
Defining what love is and what love is not
All laid out there in 1st Corinthians 13
Distilled to its essence; what it really means

Love is patient; love is kind
Slow, considerate, understanding comes to mind
Love does not boast nor fill itself with pride
A humble heart is to be glorified

Love is not rude nor seeking only self
It doesn't begin and end with trophies on the shelf
It is not easily angered; keeps no record of wrongs
Suppresses indignation like a favorite song

Love does not embrace evil, but rejoices in truth
Lies and deception just cannot take root
Love always trusts, protects, and perseveres
Starts out small, but grows with the years

And as the years pass, only three things remain
But they're all we need to be sustained
Sent from our Father, straight from above
Faith, hope, and love but the greatest is love

So when our love is challenged in new ways
Jesus set the example of how to live out our days
When our options seem to be way too few
All we need do is ask "What would love do?"

Wonderful Friends

Another year, good or bad, comes to a close
What's ahead for the New Year only God knows
Will it be one of happiness or one of despair?
One to look forward to or one to beware?

Regardless of what this next year brings
The anticipation makes our heart sing
It's as if some dark rain clouds are breaking up
And our soul is crying out, "wake up"

We start again with opportunity on a blank slate
What special occasions will we commemorate?
What precious moments will we spend with our lover?
And what great adventures will we discover?

What unfulfilled dreams will now be filled?
What tears of sorrow are yet to be spilled?
What memories will be created with family?
And what new personal horizons will we see?

What new places will we travel to and explore?
Or just reconnect with places we've been to before
Will we grow our faith or learn a new skill?
Will we sacrifice our wants in favor of God's will?

Like a transoceanic journey, we're only now leaving the dock
The year just beginning and slowly we'll unwind the clock
We've set our course, but there will be winds of change
We'll have to adapt, adjust, and our plans rearrange

There will be all kinds of challenges coming our way
But one thing I know for sure on this New Years day
As this year, with all its joys and sorrows, comes to an end
We're welcoming in this New Year with wonderful friends.

Where's the Meaning in Life?

I leave the womb, I live, and then I die
But did I ever answer the question why?
What was the purpose for being placed here on earth?
And am I fulfilling that purpose for all it's worth?

The earth was turning long before my song
And it will continue doing so long after I'm gone
I'm just a grain of sand among a billion others
What is there that's meaningful; what to discover?

The rivers run to the oceans and back again
The way they've been doing for years on end
The earth continues revolving to record the years
The sun sets; then hurries along to reappear

The planets' motion is choreographed to perfection
Their precise pattern hasn't changed since inception
It all fits together flawlessly like chapter and verse
Is there anything at all that's new in this universe?

So where do I fit in, this small speck on history
If it's all master-planned, what's the plan for me?
Can I really accomplish anything; make a difference?
When my life is over, will it have any significance?

I've tried everything to find some bit of happiness
I thought it would come with business success
I loved that new car while it was shiny and in style
But the shine disappeared in just a short little while

I tried the proverbial wine, women, and song
But that too grew old and tiring before too long
My man-toys have all lost their charm and luster
None of it has been fulfilling or passed the muster

The man upstairs has quietly let me go my way
Knowing that I would have these questions someday
But lately, He's been speaking louder into both ears
That my focus has been misdirected all these years

You see it was He who made me and He has a plan
He's been counting on me ever since time began
To boldly proclaim His message to a lost generation
So all in my circle of influence receive revelation

There's a spiritual battle going on every day
And there's a part my Lord wants me to play
Go and make disciples of all nations is the call
And my part is significant to that effort after all

He sent His Son to provide meaning to my life
To find that meaning all I had to do was accept Christ
I know what my purpose is, my mission to fulfill
It's to know my Lord and follow His will

I pray that I will be able to lead the life He wants me to
Knowing that only He can make all things new
So that when the Father comes to take me home
I'll know that the meaning in life comes from Him alone.

Whose Feet Will You Wash Today?

Why do we have such a struggle with pride versus humility?
Why do we equate passing credit to others with a loss of dignity?
Is pride part of our human sin nature, somehow built into our DNA?
Or do we learn it, episode by episode—piecemeal, day by day?

Maybe it's some of each, but I know it starts at an early age
Who can run the fastest, throw the ball the farthest, upstage
We want our achievements rewarded with higher marks and praise
Taking our rightful place on the podium, basking in those glorious rays

We instill in our children the importance of confidence
But, at what point, does confidence cross over to arrogance?
When does the home-run trot turn into obnoxious swagger?
When playing together, as a team, is all that should matter

Being competitive is not wrong until it becomes all about me
And the flames of pride are fanned every day by society
World-class athletes claiming they're the greatest of all time
And politicians taking credit for accomplishments of every kind

We are taught that we can make it happen; it's within our control
Step up to the plate; you don't need anyone, just set your goal
And when we achieve, we naturally take the credit we believe is our due
Even though it was the contribution of others that brought us through

The TV commercials belt out extravagant claims night and day
But when we try their products they either don't work or they're just OK
Every claim seems to come with a strong measure of hyperbole
And it's not tempered at all by even a hint of humility

We're quick to take credit for any kind of accomplishment or success
And just as quick to distance ourselves from association with the rest
We don't even think of what drives us this way or question why
It just seems natural to start each sentence with the pronoun "I"

And yet we have wonderful examples of humility right at hand
Consider the greatest modern-day pastor, evangelist Billy Graham
He says he has nothing to offer thousands when he begins to preach
And without the power of the Holy Spirit that he'd have nothing to teach

Then there's the apostle Paul, probably the greatest disciple of all time
Time after time, in deference to Christ, he put his life on the line
Advising his followers to value others above self
Putting their own interests on hold to offer others help

The most astounding example of humility to ever be found
Is at the Last Supper with the Apostles gathered round
When the most famous meal had begun, but was not yet complete
The God of the universe lowered himself to wash his disciples' feet

Humility may not be as difficult, after all, as it would seem to be
Perhaps we can make a start by beginning our sentences with "we"
Soon we'll see that using this technique is not only better, but preferred
And that despite what our culture teaches, humility is not a dirty word.

It will not be an easy thing to do solely through the efforts of self
It will take the power of the Holy Spirit to put Pride on the shelf
So take the next step to prevent Pride from having its way
Metaphorically speaking, whose feet will you wash today?

When

When you've kept your head as all about
Run in circles, scream, and shout
When you, in peace, have stood your ground
While the world was collapsing all around

When you've held steadfast in values, no matter the cost
Taken a stance on issues all but lost
Yet not being resistant to a time for change
As fresh ideas arise and old ones wane

When you've shown intelligence deeper than most
Yet never flaunted it nor hinted at boast
When the answer was so clear, but you didn't mind
Explaining the whole concept to us one more time

When you've walked with Kings and paupers with equal finesse
Knowing only the right stuff can truly impress
That the real deal quietly puts to shame
The age of image and inflated claim

When you've been through the business wars and yet survived
With your dignity in tact, your soul still alive
When business associates, both near and far
Admire not only your work, but who you are

When you've instilled in your family these very same traits
Never party to pity, jealousy, or hate
Work hard, work smart - keys to success
A kind heart and gentle spirit bring happiness

When you've accomplished all that you set out to do
Yet eagerly immerse yourself in a challenge brand new
Filling each day with equal measures of work and fun
That's when people will acknowledge what a man you've become.

White as Snow

It's disgusting when I look out and see trash everywhere
Walls painted with graffiti; not an empty space to spare
Beer bottles and tire rubber strewn along the road
And yards overgrown as if there's no neighborhood code

Just when you think that it's always going to be this way
The heavens rain down with an awesome display
Like a worn-down shack that transforms to a chateau
The world is renewed with a fresh blanket of snow

There's nothing quite as cleansing as new fallen snow
For a few hours, it puts a mask on all the ugliness below
Mother Nature, untouched by even one set of tracks
Glistens with a beauty and softness humanity lacks

It may be cold outside, but the snow warms the heart
All things are made fresh and the world gets a new start
All you can do is step back and admire a world made new
It's energizing and uplifting through and through

It brings back memories of when you were a child
Snowball fights, snow angels, and all the smiles
For just a while, setting aside all the ugly
Making even the cold seem warm and cuddly

That's what God's grace is like, raining down on us
Soft and invigorating like a blanket of freshly fallen snow
It covers all our shortcomings, transgressions, and sins
The ugly is painted white, with another chance to begin

Our Lord's death on the cross was an ugly testament to man
He said they know not what they do; they don't understand
But He provided a way for us and only now do we know
That when we come to him, we're seen white as snow.

You May Be the Answer to Someone's Prayer

Life on this planet can have its share of troubled times
The peace and joy we so cherish may be hard to find
We may be at a point so low that only a miracle will do
We're down on our knees begging for a breakthrough

And just when it seems things could not get any worse
That we're under the spell of some kind of curse
There's a knock at the door with the answer in hand
An answer so unexpected, it's hard to understand

It's true God can do miracles without any help from man
But sometimes He needs us to help fulfill His plan
There's a part He wants you to play for someone you know
You're the hands and feet, with the seed to sow

The need may be something picked up at the store
Or maybe it's just some simple yard-work chore
For someone who's sick, it's preparing a meal
Just listening to someone's story can be a big deal

Maybe it's a visit to someone in hospital care
A few minutes from your day can do wonders there
You don't need to bring flowers or fancy stuff
Your mere presence is more than enough

Maybe it's a prayer that's needed on this occasion
The words need not be perfect or a long invocation
The Lord already knows the nature of the request
And whatever His answer, you know it will be blessed

Maybe it's someone who's lost a spouse or a child
And have lost sight of any reason to smile
Their wonderful life has fallen into shell shock
They don't know they may just need a walk and talk

Maybe they're struggling with their faith in this mad rush
And they've permanently seated themselves on the struggle bus
There a seat beside them reserved for you
And you are the one who can pull them through

You may not think you're the right one for the task
But God thinks so or He wouldn't have asked
You may not have a clue what your next step should be
But the God of Creation will give you the vision to see

So step out of your comfort zone when He issues the call
There's someone who desperately needs you after all
Step to the front of the line and show you care
You may be the answer to someone's prayer.

You Say, I Say

You say there is no God
That he's a figment of our imagination
That our beliefs are organized fraud
A means to control our population

I say then how do you explain creation
Why is there such order to the planets and stars?
That the Big Bang is an inadequate explanation
As to how we came to be and who we are

You say the Bible is just another book
One that's human created, not divinely inspired
A lot of nice stories, but mostly gobbledygook
That it's far-fetched and never really transpired

I say the Bible is meaningless without the Holy Spirit
God's Word doesn't come alive with a casual glance
Without divine help, it will seem incoherent
Only with study will understanding have a chance

You say we need to separate church and state
That we cannot have religion in our government
That we don't need God in order to legislate
Or determine which rules will receive our consent

I say our forefathers had a different concern
More worried about the state dictating our faith
Coming from a dictatorship, they had learned
That freedom of worship was not up for debate

You say there is no heaven and there is no hell
There's no spiritual battle between evil and good
Only believe that which your eyes or ears can tell
Everything else is just nonsense and misunderstood

I say I'm concerned with what happens after this life
And this is what I believe after all that I've read
If I'm right, you'll spend eternity in agony and strife
If you're right, all that will happen is I'll be dead.

Wildflower

The seed finds its resting place where it can
Carried there by animal, wind, or man
It might find fertile soil or only rock
Obligated, though, to wait in dry dock

Then one day the rains come pouring down
The transformation begins below the ground
Seedling pokes through at the appointed hour
And in all its glory bursts forth the wildflower

One is followed by two; then quickly a score
In short order, they fill an acre or more
Red, golden, and blue compose the scheme
We stand in awe, marveling at the scene

Christians are formed in much the same way
A seed is planted by someone one day
It may or may not find a receptive soul
A hardened heart cannot accept the role

Then one day lightning strikes a spiritual cord
Maybe the right person or just the right word
Maybe it's a tragedy or a friend's advice
That sprouts a new believer in Christ

Unsure of his faith, just a fledgling at first
But strengthened by God and Bible verse
The Holy Spirit comes and the growth's complete
Like the wildflower, an aroma pure and sweet

But that's only the beginning of this odyssey
Disciple follows disciple in this new ministry
The brothers meet often to fellowship and pray
And strengthen each other in following the Way

Their numbers grow daily as others want to be
With the Lord, as He promised, for all eternity
And when the Lord looks down from his Heavenly tower
It's more pleasing to Him than any wildflower.

Your Story Matters

Jesus' instructions to his apostles were very clear
Go and make disciples of all the earth, far and near
This is what we're called to do, the Christian vision
But how do I do my part for the Great Commission?

I'm not a biblical scholar and my memory's not very good
If I need to quote some pertinent verse, I'm not sure I could
My prayers are well-intended, but often disjointed
If you're looking for Billy Graham, you'll be disappointed

But if you think back to those people God was able to use
They definitely were not the type to make the evening news
They were people like fishermen of ordinary skill and means
A willing teenager, a tax collector, and a shepherd boy extreme

Why wouldn't God have recruited a great orator or a king?
Someone who could captivate, add a measure of zing
I think it's because power is corrupting if it doesn't come from Him
And pride is one of the most difficult of the seven deadly sins

So you see, even with our limitations, we're a great asset
You won't know that until you see the table He's set
He'll provide you with the special connection you'll need
And do the rest of the work, if you just plant the seed

You have a unique story and no one knows it better than you
And in the telling, what you have in common will come through
Bringing someone to Christ may be the ultimate end
But it all starts, first and foremost, with making a friend

Maybe your story will strengthen a faith that's weak
And it will be re-energized by the words you speak
God will be more than pleased from His throne on High
That, even with all your shortcomings, you gave it a try

In witnessing for Christ, don't try to be someone you're not
It won't matter what you remembered or what you forgot
God will provide and you won't need biblical swagger
Just get started and know that your story matters.

About the Author

Jim Tayburn grew up on a dairy farm in central New York State, and while he still treasures the values that such a life instills, he knew he wanted something more. He left for the University of Buffalo and never looked back. His 37 year sales and marketing career with Occidental Petroleum took Jim and his wife, Marie, to Michigan, St. Louis, and Philadelphia, as well as Buffalo. They have witnessed firsthand the cultural and geographical landscape of living in the United States and feel blessed to have done so.

Jim and Marie retired to Tucson, Arizona in 2005 and fell in love with the beauty and amazing diversity of life in the Sonoran Desert. They have two daughters and three grandchildren who live in the East. Jim says that if there is one downside to living out West, it's the miles of separation from family.

His favorite poets are Robert Frost and Rudyard Kipling because their poems, "The Road Not Taken" and "If" are classics with a message that is simple and profound at the same time.